Property
Next Generation

C000205275

Preparing your family for a wealthy future

—— VICKI WUSCHE ——

SRA Books

Property for the Next Generation: Preparing your family for a wealthy future
© Vicki Wusche 2012
ISBN 978-1-909116-01-6

Published in 2012 by SRA Books

Printed in the UK by TJ International, Padstow

Vicki Wusche
The Shed
St Peters Road
Uxbridge, UB8 3SB

Vicki@ThePropertyMermaid.com
Skype: Vicki.Wusche
www.ThePropertyMermaid.com
www.TheSourcersApprentice.com

Liability disclaimer

The information contained in this book has been gathered and collated from the experiences of the author. Every effort has been made to make sure the details are accurate. However, they are experiences and by that nature, and the fact that they have been gathered into a book, means that they will be in the past as you read this.

It is vital that you take this information and check its relevancy to your personal situation and to the market place right now. We have been through four of the most unprecedented years in the economy, all rulebooks have been torn up and no one knows what the future holds. It is the lessons of the present that carry us forward.

Please take this information, learn from the mistakes, benefit from the successes and, above all, carve your own future in the shape you desire. Deals are easy to find but hard to buy without finance; identify your personal sources of finance and build a cashflow portfolio now.

Acknowledgements

The list of amazing people, great friends and inspiring business mentors that have helped me could fill an entire book. I really appreciate all the people that kindly agreed to be mentioned as case studies in this book: Kimberley my daughter of course, Lorraine and Ruby, Duncan and Laura, and many others.

To my family, darling Bob, Kimberley and Charlie, all my supportive family and friends – I am so proud of you all. Loran, my business partner and dear friend for keeping me on track what would I do without you?

My business mentors and peers, this year, have come in the form of Daniel Priestley, Andrew Priestley, Mike Harris, Shaa Wasmund, Penny and Thomas Power, Darren Shirlaw and all the team at Entrevo and all my friends at Key Person of Influence – now too many to name individually but you know who you are especially the "7s".

I would like to thank everyone that has worked with me either through my sourcing business, as a mentee or those who needed clarity through a strategy session.

Then last but not least my business, marketing and publishing team. Sue Richardson is consummately professional, supportive and full of technical and strategic advice – this is my third book with her and her team and I extend my thanks to all the excellent people at SRA publishing.

I have also had the fun and privilege of working with Liz Harwood of EHC who has been helping me raise my speaking profile and refine my brand.

To everyone that has helped and supported me, I am honoured to know you, grateful for your time, thoughts, contributions and care, and above all your friendship – thank you.

Contents

Foreword   vii

What people are saying about *Property for the Next Generation*   ix

Introduction   1

Chapter 1 Recognising your financial landscape   9

Chapter 2 The seven myths about money that will disadvantage your
               children for life   19

Chapter 3 The seven most important financial lessons you will ever learn 37

Chapter 4 What do you want in your life and how much will it cost?   71

Chapter 5 Teach your 22-year-old to buy their first house   77

Appendix   My story and how I learnt what school will never teach you   93

Bibliography   103

Moving forward   105

Vicki Wusche   107

The Property Sourcers   111

The Sourcer's Apprentice   113

Foreword

As a digital entrepreneur I am painfully aware of the social digital world and its impact on economies and individuals. I can see how the lives of our generation and those that go after us are very different to the world I grew up in. There is no security or comfort blanket now. The new world requires us to consider our future more than ever, securing it ourselves and relying on no one else. Building income is important, but never has it been more important to learn how to build sustainable assets.

I feel compelled to do what I can each day to build a better future not only for today's entrepreneurs, but for all our future digital generations. I do this through my work with the Digital Youth Academy, but when I saw and read Vicki's thoughts and the practical financial advice she provides, I was more than happy to add my endorsement. While I may have screwed up when it comes to property, I am determined that others don't. Reading this book makes me feel that if only I had been mentored by Vicki earlier in my life I would have made some major changes in the way I managed my income and assets early on. We are a generation of change. More and more of our economy will be built by entrepreneurs, people who build personal business assets rather than corporate business.

In these pages, Vicki challenges our thoughts surrounding property and money. She questions whether we are using our investments wisely and questions whether our home is our castle, or just a heavy liability that we pass on to our children. How do we teach them to use an asset as a way to leverage income, and how do we ensure our children go forward never having to experience the financial concerns our generation have experienced.

Vicki's book has been eye opening and revealing, and has certainly given me an insightful indication of how to move forward.

Penny Power
www.DigitalYouthAcademy.com
@PennyPower

What people are saying about
Property for the Next Generation

Vicki's book is a vital wake up call for parents who are prepared to challenge the current economic situation and who are behind making a positive change for the future. By considering our future generations in the way we invest money today, we can use this dynamic time of entrepreneurial revolution to make those changes. Well done Vicki in bringing this to the attention of parents globally.

Daniel Priestley, author of *Becoming a Key Person of Influence*
www.entrevo.com

As a parent, property investor and creative entrepreneur, I believe everyone with an interest in bettering their own and their children's lives should read Vicki's book. Anyone with a desire to do what they love but are unable to because they are shackled by the J.O.B and the schlep to work every day should start following Vicki's strategies. Like Vicki, I started a journey of financial awakening in 2008 after reading *The Cashflow Quadrant* (Kiyosaki). In 2009 I felt the fear and bought my first investment property anyway, continuing to buy several more over the next two years. This allowed me a quality of life I could only dream of two years ago. Vicki demystifies property investment and encourages her readers to take personal responsibility for their own futures. Start planning your corporate escape now by following Vicki's strategies and give your teenager a copy of this book too. It is never too early to train them on how they can get the life they deserve. You'd be mad to let your family's financial future slip to the bottom of your to do list.

Lorraine Stylianou
www.gypsy-chic.co.uk

Everyone should read this book because every decent parent wants the best for their child(ren) and may want to give it to them in the form of material things. This knowledge and practical advice will not only provide the parent with a system to enable them to afford these provisions but set them and their children and indeed the following generation up for life to provide for themselves in financial terms plus aim for and achieve the life they want.

Bella King
www.bellakingsolutions.com

This book is an absolute must for anyone that has children or even those who don't but do have an under-performing pension. This book highlights the very real financial issues facing our next generation and a concise strategy for securing the financial freedom they deserve. As I read through the book, things I thought I knew suddenly made a lot more sense and I can now clearly see a way through the monetary minefield.

This is a book the whole country needs to know about, an extremely enjoyable and thought provoking read. Lorraine Kelly and Alan Titchmarsh are surely fighting over which one of them will get Vicki on their show first.

Duncan Cooke
www.duncancookesolutions.com

Property for the Next Generation is a brilliant book on an alternative and viable way to create financial security for your family. It blows away the myths that we have swallowed as truth about our financial futures and in easy, simple language explains the property alternative. If you are worried about your family's financial future, or even just yours, then this book is a must read. Having never contemplated property investment before, this book has given me a great introduction as well as motivation to look at it for the future.

Jessica McGregor Johnson, author of *The Right T-Shirt – Write Your Own Rules and Live the Life You Want*
www.jessicamcgregorjohnson.com

Meeting Vicki has been the biggest inspiration so far for my present and future success. This latest book is so exciting to me as I see it as a summary of what she has shared with me as a client over the past 6 months, a reminder of how I have grown in this time and how she can help others to grow too. As always her straightforward style makes easy yet powerful mind-awakening reading.

Vicki demonstrates how to evaluate what is important to ourselves and how small changes can make life changing events in our lives just by thinking differently. Whilst many of us, younger people included, are starting to understand that the future looks bleak for those who are reliant only on the Government to see them through retirement, there are so many also that do not realise the answer is in their own hands. In this book, Vicki uses her skills and experience to demonstrate how individuals can actually take action and control their own life plan.

It's not always easy to convince our children to take our advice. Particularly if our own mind set has only recently changed, much of the conditioning has already taken place. Often they prefer the advice of others because it's different, interesting and optional! I see this book as a vehicle to help me and many others to bridge that gap for our children and protect their futures along with safeguarding our own.

Judith Green, Managing Director, Versatile Lift Company and mother to three daughters
www.VersatileLiftCompany.co.uk

As someone who has spent considerable time with "my head in the sand" around finances, I feel inspired by this book. Vicki shares so much more than her knowledge and personal experience around property. She shares her urgent message of a better, more responsible financial attitude, which is essential reading across the generations. I will be giving each of my four daughters a copy of this insightful and practical book asap!

Lis Allen, business owner and parent www.lisallen.com

Also by Vicki Wusche

Using Other People's Money: How to invest in property, Second Edition. SRA Books, 2012. ISBN: 978-1-909116-00-9

Make More Money from Property: From investor thinking to a business mindset. SRA Books, 2012. ISBN: 978-0-9567553-4-6

Introduction

Who are you and why are you reading this book?

As you've picked up this book, you are likely to have some or all of the following:

- A great job with a substantial income.
- A successful business that you have been running for a number of years.
- You own your own home with a relatively low mortgage.
- A family that you love, but that costs you a fortune.
- No time and more stress than you would like.
- School fees to pay.
- University fees on the horizon.
- Activities and hobbies, for you and the children.
- Savings or bonuses in the bank doing nothing.
- A pension that won't give you the retirement you want.
- A constant eye on your finances.
- You are worried about your financial future.
- Maybe an existing property portfolio that is not performing as you expected.

Above all, you know there must be a better and easier way.

Who am I and what gives me the right to write this book?

- I run two successful businesses: one teaching people how to run their own successful property businesses and the other sourcing cashflowing property for bespoke clients.

- This is my third book, I love sharing what I have learnt and achieved by applying the theory.
- I created a family portfolio worth £2 million with a £100,000 turnover in just 20 months in 2009–10.
- I have two daughters, one at university and the other in her own home that she bought with no cash from me – only my advice and support.
- Bob is my life partner, dive buddy and best friend and we spend our time enjoying life.
- I am busy, often travelling around the country speaking, but it never feels like work – I love what I do.
- I don't have a pension – I have a property portfolio.
- I don't have 'savings' – I have constant cashflow.
- I don't have to work – so effectively I am retired and doing what I love.
- I watch the markets and the economy with amazement and curiosity, not stress or worry.
- My family is well cared for.

Above all, I found a better way – I won't say it was easy, but I am now taking responsibility for my financial future and it feels much better, and the accountant tells me it *is* better.

How can you know what you don't know?

Like you, I went to school. I went to university. I achieved a first-class honours and then a Master's degree. I obtained teaching qualifications and became a university lecturer…

Yet, no one EVER discussed the implications of using a credit card, interest payments or how to buy a house. No one talked about how money really worked and how I could get it to work for me!

No one ever explained how the beliefs of my parents might be influencing the choices I was making in my life. Or that those beliefs would become a challenge, even hindrance, to my success given the dramatic rate of change happening in the financial world, business, technology and global economics.

I needed to be able to make informed decisions – not live my life by the unconscious rules and filters my parents, teachers, peers, press and even the government imposed upon me.

I never recognised, even from within the education system as a teacher that school was failing our children – the next generation. School was failing to equip my own daughters for life in a complex environment driven by global dynamics.

Luckily, I was unconsciously sharing my understanding and experience with them. My experiences, as tough as some of them were, actually helped me teach my children how to function in this debt-driven economy.

Who is teaching your children? Who is explaining to them:

- how money works
- about good debt versus bad debt
- why the rich get richer
- how working long hours in a high paid job won't make you rich or happy
- why some families seem to be able to buy property for their children and yet other families have 'children' in their 20s, 30s, even 40s still living at home
- how, as a single parent, I could help my daughter buy her own home?

In all honesty, none of these thoughts even entered my mind before 2007. Then, I gradually started to recognise and understand how and why I thought the things I did, acted the way I did, achieved (or didn't achieve) the things I wanted. I started to realise that there was more to life than I had been taught in school – considerably more.

I realised that I was not completely clueless. As a single parent with two daughters under the age of three years, I had to learn to budget the hard way. I recorded every penny I spent. I pushed my washing to the laundrette in the pram with my youngest sitting on the top as she was too little to walk such a long way. My eldest rode on the rear axle.

I worked out how I could use credit to extend my university student grant so that I could put the money in a higher interest rate account and buy what we needed on a credit card and, in doing so, effectively give myself another 56 days' money. This meant we earned £60–80 interest over the year, which paid for our summer holiday treats. I learnt that not managing your money on credit cards meant that the bank had the holiday and we did not! I started to see things differently – and to think differently.

Before 2007, it was like someone had been keeping a secret that I hadn't even known existed. Now that I knew it did exist, my next challenge was to discover exactly what it was other people knew that I did not.

- Who knew the critical secrets that would help me change my life?
- What exactly did they know?
- What was going to be important in my life and in the life of my family going forward?

What is important for you and your family moving forward?

This book will explain in plain English how you can help your child to buy property. You will not need to give them £10,000s. Instead, you will share with them your understanding of how money and the mind work from reading this book. In fact, by the time you get to the end of this book you and your child might recognise that you don't even need to own the home you live in – you just need to own cashflowing properties.

You could use property to create an income stream to increase your overall family income, or to pay for your children's private or university education. You might plan to invest in property as a retirement vehicle for yourself and your partner, or to help your children start their own businesses. What you choose will depend on your current circumstances and your future plans. This book will take you through that thinking process and, help you to shape your ideas into a personal investment plan and a cashflowing property portfolio.

Yes, I will need to talk about the mind and how you (as parents) think about money, as this is a major influencing factor on the decisions you have been making up until now. The fact is that our lives are determined by the imprints left by our parents before we even reach the age of seven! The words we heard, the way we were treated and the values our parents exhibited shaped our lives to such an extent that we have unconsciously created filters to sort through all the gigabytes of data, information and experiences we come across for the rest of our lives.

Most of us are completely unaware of these filters – I was until I started my journey into personal development. At that point I really started to understand how my mind worked. Once I understood that I recognised how much more I needed to learn. I understood why rich people get richer and ordinary people just work hard all their lives. I understood how my beliefs could help or hinder my children in their life plans.

My journey began in 2007 with understanding the mind. In 2008, I focused on learning about how money worked. By 2009, I was buying investment properties at a rate of one or two per month for myself, family and partners. By 2010, I had published my first book and I no longer had to work for a wage (I was financially free to choose how I spent my day). Finally, in 2011, my daughter bought her first house with no significant financial help from me. If you want to read more of my journey from single parent to property business entrepreneur, speaker, author and mentor (in four years), see the Appendix on page 93.

I simply shared with my daughter what I had learnt, not in school but through my own research and education, through questioning and applying the theory, by learning through practice and improving the practice. I have gone on to speak to thousands of people, teaching them how to invest in property for a more secure financial future, a life of freedom and choice that is stress free and fun. That is what this book will share with you.

This book will explain everything you need to know in order to teach your child how to buy property (everything that school failed to teach you – and them!); in other words, property and property investment for the next generation. If you think you might have access to financial resources, such as equity in your home, savings, or pensions, but are too busy to do it yourself, don't worry, I can help you buy a cashflowing portfolio that will become your income-generating asset for years to come.

What if you don't take action now?

If you don't take responsibility for your own financial future, then you will face an impoverished retirement with drastic implications for your children and grandchildren. You will leave a burden of debt and commitment as you drag out your remaining retirement years in a care home, draining them of every penny they did not have.

Notice I don't use the word 'home', in any of my explanations. The property my daughter has bought is her home, of course, but it is also just a house. I have explained to her that this property is her first investment property; bought at the best time to buy this generation will ever see. This is not about emotion; it's about business and wealth creation. Emotion is reserved for the life you live knowing you are financially secure.

Property is an incredible asset

It is tangible, in demand and controllable. We know there are not enough houses. We also know that, as an island, there are only so many houses that we can ever build in the UK. People need to live somewhere and, with a growing population, demand for property will increase. Once you own a property (with a mortgage), as long as you continue to repay your debt, you will be able to control its use and its potential to generate an additional income.

You can choose who lives there, what rent they pay, whether or not to renovate or split the property into private rooms. All of this will change as I influence your understanding of market demands and property investment as a business model. You will become more attuned to the economic environment we live in. Not the version of the economy expressed in *The Sun*, *Mirror* or *Daily Express*, but the shocking reality that we are standing on the edge of a precipice. This year will see you make decisions that will impact on your family for eternity. Are you going to take responsibility for your financial future and that of your family, or fall off the edge of the cliff like all the lemmings?

I assume that as you have bought this book, or are at least reading this book, you are already someone who realises that things need to change; that the world our children are facing is so dramatically different from our 'simple' lives and that we need to prepare them not burden or shackle them with our debt (they already have the government's debt to repay!). You are already different from the masses who just don't realise that we are in the eye of the storm. You understand that we need to prepare and take action.

The following chapters will explain how, as parents, you need to think differently about money, property investment and the future of your family. The rich will continue to get richer because they understand this stuff. This book will take you through the seven myths that our children face and the seven lessons you need to teach them.

I will explain explicit strategies step by step that you can follow to help your child buy their own house; the caveat being that they need to be over 18 years old to hold a mortgage. If your children are younger, then you can start buying houses for them now while property prices are so cheap compared to what they will be in just a few years.

Chapter 1

Recognising your financial landscape

If you are busy working long hours away from your family and don't feel rich and relaxed but you are happy with that, then maybe there is nothing wrong with the way things are. However, this whole book is written on the assumption that you are working long hours away from your family, you don't feel rich, you don't feel relaxed and you are even worried about what the future might hold financially.

To add to your worries, your private pension has dropped significantly in value as the stock market has fallen in the last 3–4 years. Your bonus accumulates in the building society or as bonds earning you nothing. The government pension can no longer be relied upon to help.

Your children will expect to leave home and get a home of their own. How will you be able to help? You will still be paying off their school and university fees. They will be paying off their university loans. So even with all this money flowing around your family you are still not rich and don't feel that your family is financially secure.

According to the papers

The press share their statistics and love to tell you how difficult it is to buy your own home. The media is telling your children from an early age that they will be 35 years old before they can have their own house. A survey by Santander bank found that a third of non-homeowners believe they will never be able to afford to buy their own property. Four out of five under-30s cannot afford to buy a home without help from their parents.[1] Are you

---

1 http://www.independent.co.uk/money/mortgages/firsttime-buyers-life-begins-at-40-6265083.html

ready to have your children live at home until they are 35 years old and then borrow a deposit from you? Well, in my experience it does not have to be like that.

In coming years the number of first-time buyers looking to step on to the property ladder will continue to drop and that's not good for the property market or parents – unless they start to rent instead. Of the 27% of the population looking to buy a home in 2012, 69% were university educated and over 30 years old.[2] If you don't act now to secure your children's future (whatever their age), it will cost you hundreds of thousands of extra pounds in years to come. Property prices will rise again and it will only get more difficult to get on to the property ladder.

But what about everyone else?

I was speaking to a group about this topic recently and one member of the audience said that it did not seem fair that I should help people to invest in property when others could not afford it. That's like saying if I saw you drowning then I shouldn't throw you a life ring or tell you how to swim, because others could not hear me!

I come from a position – a belief system – that says 'charity begins at home'. We must remember to put the oxygen mask on ourselves before we help others. We cannot afford to make excuses or to waste time. We must act now and take responsibility to secure our own family's financial future. Once we are secure we can help others. In effect, that is what I am doing. I know my mentees are all looking to coach and help others achieve what they are achieving.

In the end, not everyone will own their own home. Some people will rent from others who own a large number of properties. That is fine, not everyone owns a business. Some people are employees and are very happy with their choice. Property is the same – some people want to own and others want to rent. I will explain shortly that you won't have to live in a property that you own or own a property that you live in. As long as you

---

2   http://www.telegraph.co.uk/finance/personalfinance/borrowing/mortgages/9516916/Graduates-to-drive-return-of-first-time-buyers.html#

own a cashflowing property portfolio you will have the choice and financial security to decide what suits you best at that point in your life.

What are you doing with your money?

Perhaps you have a reasonable family income. What are you doing with your money? Well, there are a few choices:

- Overspending, including increasing your credit card debt as you live beyond your means (working 60-hour weeks neither makes you happy nor helps to make ends meet).
- Saving in a bank or building society, maybe even a bond. However, rates are so low that inflation is effectively countering any gains you might be making.
- Thinking that clearing your mortgage is a good idea.

Overspending is a straight road to disaster and financial ruin. During the late 1990s and early 2000, we were encouraged by the media, lending policies and clever marketing to become a consumerist society that absolutely had to have the latest gadget. This transferred money from your account directly into the accounts of the business owners. As the volume of debt loaned exceeded the volume of gold reserves to support it the economy started to falter.

During 1997–1998, the economic bubble burst with stories of American lenders giving loans to people who had no jobs and no income so they could live the American dream (promoted by President Bush) of owning their own home. Whatever happened to getting a job, saving up and then buying a house – the old-fashioned British method? Yet, Britain was just as bad. Northern Rock lent homebuyers 125% of the value of the house. That might have seemed okay in a climbing market and while the homeowner can afford to pay the mortgage, but we now know what happens as a result of that approach to lending.

It is crucial to review all spending habits, to teach our children about money and debt and to understand credit cards, credit scores, interest rates, etc. I cover the highlights of this in Chapter 3.

On the other hand, interest rates are at an all-time low. So saving money is a waste of time. Leaving money in an account or bond where it is earning less than the rate of inflation is like filling a bath without putting the plug in. Your money will not grow and, in real terms, will actually be worth less as the cost of living increases.

Overpaying your personal mortgage to reduce the debt is madness, unless you are over geared. If your aim is to clear your residential mortgage as fast as possible in order to live in a mortgage-free home, then you are following a misguided path. I did a calculation for a city-based lawyer as part of our discussion about him working with me. He wanted to repay his mortgage as fast as possible because, like many people, he thought it was a good idea.[3] We estimated that he and his wife could overpay their mortgage by £2,000 per month – that's £24,000 in the first year. Their aim was to remortgage their property on to a better interest rate to take advantage of the low rates that are around right now.

Potential problems:

- Would his current mortgage allow him to overpay without a penalty?
- Next year when he wants to remortgage would his current lender allow him out of his deal without penalty?
- In two years after paying off £48,000 would interest rates still be as low?

I showed him that a mortgage of approximately £240,000 on a capital and repayment mortgage of 4.99% would cost about £1,400. After 12 months of over-payments they would owe (approximately) £216,000. If they remortgaged to a lender offering, for example 3%, their monthly mortgage payment would be £1,023 – that would be a saving of £375 per month. *Yet*, the £4,500 a year saving would have cost them £24,000 to achieve, *plus* the

---

3   English Housing Survey 2009–2010 http://www.communities.gov.uk/publications/corporate/statistics/ehs200910householdreport

cost of a new survey, solicitor costs, broker fees and maybe even penalties from the first lender.

Does this make sense to you?

They don't have children yet, but what if they took that £24,000 (added another £6,000) and bought a buy-to-let property in the north of England and rented it out to a family? After expenses they could expect to achieve about £250 per month rental profit. That's £3,000 a year, this year, next year and ongoing, plus 25% equity in another property that will increase in future value.

While the thought of saving £4,500 on your mortgage compared to earning £3,000 from an investment property might seem like a good idea, the £3,000 comes with an advantage – 25% or more equity in another property. After seven years, for example, you would still owe over £100,000 including interest on your mortgage. You would have spent £168,000 and saved less than £30,000.

If you bought an investment property portfolio of six or more properties, you could have an annual additional income (profit) of £18,000 – that's £126,000 income over the seven years – compared to £30,000 in savings. Plus you would own equity in those properties of an additional £150,000–200,000!

The city lawyer and I are now discussing how I can help him to invest in a portfolio of cashflowing property that will give him between 10–20%[4] return on his investment.

The average person in England still wants to own their own house

The average person is still striving for some past ideal where an 'Englishman's home is his castle'. Some say it started with Margaret Thatcher's ideals, but I know that my parents held those beliefs some 20–30 years before she came into power.

---

4   10–20% to allow for variation in property type, location and interest rates based on your credit worthiness.

As a country, we have this conflict between feeling that our 'home is our castle' and yet seemingly being priced out of the housing market. Watch the video from Shelter,[5] which brilliantly explains in under three minutes using a simple cartoon how the housing market went bang.

The best thing about viewing property as a professional property investor is that I understand I neither need to own the home I live in nor live in any of the homes I own. However, the property that we do own must pay for us to live rent free in a home of our choice. This means that the implied challenge for first-time buyers of stepping up on to an unaffordable housing ladder is removed. Instead of buying where you want to live, invest where you can afford and let the rental profit pay for you to rent where you want.

Let me explain this further so that you can start to detach yourself from beliefs that served your parents in a post-war Britain.

We already know that our lives are becoming more mobile. We move for work, for pleasure or out of aspiration; few stay put because of family ties. The lives of our children will be driven by their desire and need to be more mobile, more flexible and generally less attached to one physical place.

They may start by needing to relocate for study, then for work and eventually, when love strikes, for family reasons, but with technological advances they are more likely to move out of choice. So the dilemma of where they will call their home needs addressing in another way. What if you could have the benefit of feeling secure without the burden and obligation of a residential mortgage on a property that may no longer suit your needs?

What if you or your children (over the age of 18) owned a number of properties in a part of the country where the rental income was high in proportion to the purchase cost of the property? What if the rental income gave you the flexibility and choice to live wherever you wanted? So, while you are young, single and working in London you choose to live in a flat in London. Then, as you meet a partner, settle down and start a family you want a garden so you move. Finally, as you retire you move to the coast. And all without the cost and stress of selling a single property!

---

5   Shelter video http://bit.ly/Shelter-Vid

There is a challenge with renting

Part of the challenge with renting, as a tenant in the UK, is that we use six-month AST (assured shorthold tenancy) agreements as our contractual agreement, as developed through the housing acts of 1980, 1988 and 1996.[6]

In Germany, for example, the majority of property is rented accommodation (90% in Berlin and 80% in Hamburg[7]). The primary contract gives a German tenant an unlimited contract to rent and even if notice is given by a landlord a tenant can still appeal to stay. Combined with the lack of appreciable rise in house values, this makes for a much more stable and secure housing market. Tenants have rights around rental increases and compared with London it's almost 50% cheaper to rent in Munich.[8]

For the average tenant in the UK, the message is: 'Live here for a while – I don't expect you to stay long because this is not really your home.' It is no wonder that private renting is only at 20%. Whereas in Germany the message is: 'Stay as long as you want – you are welcome.' Needless to say, in the UK, properties can often be treated as temporary homes, maintenance costs can be high and turnover, especially in London, is expected. In Germany, tenants are expected to pay for the cost of redecoration.

If you add the fact that the German housing market has only risen about 2–3% in the last 10 years compared to UK house prices almost doubling, then maybe the problems with the housing market is less to do with Margaret Thatcher, ASTs or anything else and plainly just to do with property speculation and mad lending policies.

How can we change the view of renting?

Well, we need to separate the idea of owning properties and living in a home. Yes, we do still have a bit of a challenge in the UK with the AST contract, but conversations among the professional landlords would all report the same fact: 'We would love a long-term secure tenant.'

---

6   http://www.housinglaw.org.uk/AST.htm

7   http://www.guardian.co.uk/money/2011/mar/19/brits-buy-germans-rent

8   http://www.guardian.co.uk/money/2011/mar/19/brits-buy-germans-rent

Maybe I am jumping ahead with radical ideas a bit too soon – I just want to shake up the way you think and say it doesn't have to be like that for our children. If you start now, you could create a cashflowing portfolio of properties that generates additional income for the family. Depending on your needs, it could fund school fees, university fees, a deposit for a house, pay the rent on a city pad for your city-working offspring or fund your retirement.

It can be done. I will show you examples: one where you can take control – especially if your children are under 18 and therefore not yet eligible for a mortgage. I will also show you how you can help your teenager prepare to buy their own home, or property portfolio, as soon as they get a full-time job and pass the legal requirements to hold a mortgage. I will explain to you in easy-to-follow steps how I taught my daughter to buy her own £200,000 house in Greater London in November 2011 with no money from the 'bank of Mum and Dad'. And the house is fully furnished, decorated and complete with two cats!

I will share case studies of friends and clients who, as parents, are already helping their children to think differently about property. I will explain how their whole way of thinking has changed, and how it is rippling out to wider family members. I will show you how these young people have started down the path to buy their own property portfolios. I will show you how I am helping people with good incomes recognise how they can become even more wealthy by working with me to buy a cashflowing property portfolio.

Since the start of 2009, I have bought enough houses that I no longer need to work to earn money. I have used this experience to help bespoke clients to buy investment properties that have enabled them to do everything from give up work and start designing children's books to emigrate to a life in the sun leaving behind a portfolio of cashflowing properties that takes care of the family in their absence.

I regularly speak at both property and business-related events, sharing my knowledge and understanding. As more people asked me to help them, I started to write books (this is my third). Now I mentor a small number of private clients to grow their business in property or commerce. The bulk of my business is helping people to invest in cashflowing portfolios.

Throughout everything I do, my passion for life and learning is, I believe, evident. I love to share my knowledge; my books, talks and businesses enable me to do this.

Alongside my passion for life is my passion for Bob my partner of 13+ years and our shared interest in scuba diving and underwater photography. So, holidays and travel are a big part of our lives. In the last couple of years, we have travelled to Egypt, the Maldives, the Philippines, Thailand, Sulawesi and the freezing cold Bristol Channel. My speaking has taken me to Preston in Lancashire, Hull, Exeter and Ipswich, with Birmingham, Brighton and London in between. I have spoken at the Business Shows in Excel and Olympia, and to groups of entrepreneurs. Wherever we go, Bob and I plan to add a day or two for ourselves to explore and relax.

We don't have to work a 60-hour week to make ends meet. We have the income that gives us the freedom to choose to live our lives on our terms.

My two daughters are settled at university and in work. They have comfortable homes. My parents are comfortable and well cared for. My life is truly wonderful. Best of all, I made every decision that brought me to this point. I recognised in late 2007 that I needed to take responsibility for my life and it was going to be fun all the way. Most importantly, when the time to slow down does eventually arrive I will not be a burden on my children. I will not compound their debt. I will not limit their lives by making them sell everything they have to pay for my living costs.

We have been repeatedly fed the same myths – by school, the government, the media and unknowingly by our parents. It's time to get the truth out into the open and really start to recognise the mess the economy is in – and us with it! It's time to take steps to secure your financial future now you know where you stand.

Let me ask you some questions as a way to summarise what I have covered already:

- Do you have children or want children and worry about how they will ever be able to afford to get on the housing ladder?
- Do you work hard and earn a good wage, yet there is never enough… enough time, enough money, enough fun?
- Are you worried that you don't have a private pension and, even if you do, that it will not be worth enough to support you in your retirement?
- Do you wish you could do something different, but can't afford to leave your job?
- Are you worried you might lose your job?
- Would you just like to know how you can feel more relaxed about money, feel wealthier and feel positive about the future?

If you have answered yes to any of these questions, then investing in a cashflowing property portfolio could be the perfect solution. This and my other books can help.

Chapter 2 will unpack some of the myths that I believe are holding us back from a simpler and more secure financial future. A future that is secure because it is *not* blown by the wind of banking speculation, whether property or stock based. A future that is secure because as we become more successful and wealthy, we help others, reinvest in the economy and put fuel into the economic engine rather than watch it jerk through a repeating cycle of boom and bust.

As parents, we need to understand that the lives, learning styles, demands on, working conditions and priorities of our children are so very different to our lives. The speed of information, their ability to multi-process, working practices changing dramatically with technological advances and the dangerous state of our debt-ridden world economy all mean that the chances of your grandchildren living a comfortable and secure life is guaranteed to be minute – unless you start making the changes NOW!

As you read on through the following pages leave your old ways of thinking behind. Be open to new ideas and new ways of doing things. This is not just for you but for your children and your family – you need to understand how everything is changing and how you can prepare.

Chapter 2

The seven myths about money that will disadvantage your children for life

Myth 1: we don't need to know how money works – we have jobs

Fact: you must understand how money works. Anyone who does not is heading for financial disaster

In fact, you need to think of yourself as a business, and then your children will also start to think that way. What are your skills and how are you selling them? You may sell your skills to another person as an employee or contractor – it is just a variation on a theme. Or perhaps you are selling an idea (as a product, concept or service) as a business owner with employees, contractors or outsourced staff.

Your children will need to think like this because the idea of a job for life will not exist. With the average student leaving university with between £26,000 and £32,000 of debt[9] and 25% of them joining the dole queue, it all seems mad. The smart ones will be getting online and working out how they can sell something (an idea, a skill or their time) to someone else.

So what does this have to do with needing to know how money works? I believe we all need to think like business owners. We need to know the value of our time or skill. We need to maximise the return we get for that exchange either in terms of money, flexibility, stability, status or other values that are important to us. We need to understand how to survive and provide – to survive in a world built on debt and provide for our families. And by that I mean to provide not just the cash resources but the knowledge and understanding that traditional education will simply not teach our children.

---

9   http://bit.ly/NUS-Funding

Do you understand why you got turned down for a loan or had a credit card limit reduced? If this has not happened to you, do you understand why it is happening to others and what you need to do to avoid that same fate?

What do your children understand about money, credit and the real cost of interest payments? Do they understand good debt versus bad debt? If school has not explained this, then how can they be expected to function in today's business world?

Do you realise the impact that one missed mobile phone payment can have on your child's future ability to buy a property? Managing your credit scores and even your online reputation is crucial if you are to be even more successful in the coming years.

Truth

We cannot carry on blindly following the advice offered in school which is blatantly inappropriate.

1. Buy a house on a mortgage and live happily ever after. *You can't.*
2. Rely on the government to keep you safe, fed and housed – there is plenty of money. *There is not.*
3. Debt is good. *It is not good if it is spent on liabilities rather than assets.*
4. Your pension will be fine – just save more. *It will never be enough.*
5. Go to university and get a good job. *No, you won't. You will just get another £30,000 of debt to pay off (with no job to help). No wonder you will have to move home and live with Mum and Dad!*

Myth 2: the government will take care of you

Fact: with an ageing and expanding population, there just is not enough money to go round!

Since the introduction of Beveridge's welfare state in 1942,[10] the government has been driven by the need to take care of us. Each successive government over the last 70 years has worked even harder to give us the impression that it can afford this commitment.

Beveridge's aim was noble and politically astute. The country needed a healthy, educated population living in decent housing that could go out and do a hard day's work getting the nation and the economy back on its feet after the devastating human and financial cost of the Second World War. So, creating jobs through a national health service (NHS), free education system, planned building works and various other government bodies, increased employment generating a flow of money, which stimulated the economy.

The rebalancing of the economy came at a cost: income support (unemployment benefit, sick benefit), free education, free housing, free health... prescriptions, glasses, dentistry, operations and general health practitioners – the cost was enormous.

During 2009–2010 the government *spent* £671.4 billion despite tax *revenues* of only £496.1 billion.[11] Under current spending plans, the national debt could well top 79% of GDP by 2014. Ironically, the last time we borrowed this much money was to fund the Second World War.

The downside in economic terms of a more healthy population living longer, because of the free and life-prolonging treatments on the NHS, is the burden on the other social services. As adult mortality decreased, the average age that men and women lived to increased.

After the Second World War, when the state pension age was 65 years for men, their life expectancy was 66.4 years, while women's was 72.5 years. In fact, men today typically live to 77, while the figure is 82 for women. By

---

10 http://www.bbc.co.uk/schools/gcsebitesize/history/mwh/britain/welfarestaterev1.shtml

11 http://www.debtbombshell.com/public-spending.htm

2056, the life expectancy for a man and woman living in England is expected to be 84 and 89 respectively.[12]

For the first time in history, with Britain's over 65 population outnumbering the under 16 year olds, there is a bad omen for future tax revenues – a sure sign of even greater budgetary problems ahead if we maintain this course of a subsidised existence.

Therefore, an original idea designed to help the general population resulted in more people living longer, requiring even more treatments on the NHS and more pension payments, which in turn meant more spending.

The benefit system, which was designed to support those most in need, in fact created a culture of expectation and dependency amongst generations to follow. In my experience, I have met many young people who are part of a long line of unemployed and disadvantaged families – often with parents who are separated, poor and suffering from addictions. I was tempted to say that they lack motivation, but that's not accurate; they lack *something to be motivated about* – the possibilities in their lives have been limited by their parents' and grandparents' lack of employment. This new generation of young parents is no more capable of holding down a job or teaching their children about a bright new future than their grandparents were.

Some young people develop the belief, through the media and peer pressure, that reliance on the state is acceptable. Many live on the edge of a black economy. Those with entrepreneurial skills learn to survive on benefits by identifying ways to generate additional income and opportunities. They have found a way to survive that effectively empowers them rather than leaving them feeling powerless and impoverished by the benefit system. The majority of young people are entrepreneurial and creative but through a series of life events do not feel empowered to work within the system and don't recognise that relying on the benefit system is part of their problem.

The costs of all these outbound payments are met by taxes and when the potential burden of tax required is too high the government resorts to

---

12 http://www.dailymail.co.uk/news/article-2128540/Raise-retirement-age-save-British-economy-IMF-warning-crippling-cost-pensions.html

borrowing. This becomes our national debt. Just as in a family unit, if you keep spending (on pensions and NHS, free education and unemployment benefits) more than you are earning (through taxes) and then you resort to borrowing (or creating more 'cash' through fiscal measures) with no clear plan to repay the debt, you will soon be in trouble.

So what does the myth that 'government will take care of you' mean to us and, more importantly, our children? Debt and disaster, unemployment and global recession, no money, hunger, civil unrest? This will have to come to a horrible end as the world's economy simply cannot go on borrowing money that does not exist indefinitely. Greece is a perfect example of this madness; because they cannot pay their debt, Europe lends them more money... surely this madness is evident?

This book is not designed to solve the political or financial problems looming on the horizon, it is here to help you recognise the potential impact on your family and how you can make changes now to set course for a more financially secure future.

In truth, all you need to know in this context is that you will have to start doing things differently. You and your children will have to take responsibility for your own financial futures and then, when you have mastered your own financial situation, help those around you.

There is a growing culture that desires change and a new way, rather than a black market or a grey economy, which I would say is a silver lining to this storm-laden economic cloud. People are coming together in partnerships to lend one another money in a different way. Why leave your money in the bank if you could lend it to a family member or friend and get better interest, or even a reward in another format? That is how I bought part of my property portfolio.

'Dragons' Den' style and 'Angel' funding is an obvious example of how to borrow money without going to the bank. Thanks to technology and the rate of innovation, objects, services and ways of doing business are changing rapidly. Individuals are finding how technology can help them get their projects funded and others are finding a more satisfying return for their savings than the paltry 2–3% in the banks. Online environments like Crowdcube and BanktotheFuture.com enable people to lend money to one another. Why pay 4000%[13] from these quick money lenders advertised on TV or the underground? Everything that our parents took for granted (including a job for life and a guaranteed pension to live on) has changed.

Truth

The government is going bankrupt trying to pay for an ideal promise made 70 years ago. It is unsustainable. The truth is that pensions will be worth nothing in the future whether you are relying on a state pension or a private pension. You need to act now and secure a financial future for your family.

Myth 3: work hard, buy your home and live happily ever after

Fact: you will have to sell your home to afford to eat; your home is not an asset

I don't know if I explicitly learnt this at school or if it was implied by my parents, but I expected to get a job, buy a house on a mortgage, pay it off over the next 25 years and live happily ever after. Maybe it was just a fairy tale I read in a book.

Even as I worked for a mortgage company in my early married life, I could see that the model I described above didn't work. House buyers needed to take out a 'savings/life' policy called an endowment that would mature and pay out a lump sum designed to clear the mortgage debt because the monthly payments required were too high when calculated over a 25-year term.

This was because mortgage affordability was high. It has got much worse. Back in 1983, the affordability ratio was 3:5, meaning the average property (£31,203) cost 3.5 times the average salary (£8,902). By 2007, the average

---

13 An advert seen on the London Underground offering pay day loans at that exorbitant interest rate.

house price was £199,084 and that represented over 5.8 times the average person's salary (£34,252).

Average property prices doubled from £31,203 to £68,623 in just seven years (by 1990). By 2003, 13 years later it had doubled again to £132,371. In 2003 to 2007 (just four years) average property prices rose by 150% to £199,084.[14] This meant property was increasing in cost by £45.69 a day! £1,370.82 a month!

The financial crisis means that some people are changing their mortgage products from capital and repayment (the traditional way to pay off some of your debt and some of the cost in each monthly payment) to interest-only payments to reduce the monthly cost, as they struggle to make ends meet. This means that they are paying a mortgage on a property that they will never own, because 10 or 20 years from now they will still owe the same debt. They are gambling that high prices will rise and interest rates stay low enough so that they can avoid repossession!

Ironically, I use that same method to buy my property portfolio, expecting property inflation to increase the price of the house and effectively reduce the debt, but at least I do it knowingly and as part of a business plan that generates cashflow for me and my family, rather than thinking I own a house but actually I am just a high rent paying tenant of a bank!

As I started to work with my clients to help them buy property that would generate an income – giving them choice and security – I began to see an equation forming.

Along your lifeline starting with birth and ending with death – the only two certainties in life – you will most likely get a job and buy a house. We already know from historical data that house prices go up and even double in most cases in just over 7–10 years.

So, let's say you own your house worth £300,000 now and maybe it takes 10 years to double. In 2023, or thereabouts, your house could be worth £600,000. Your children will have left home and you might be thinking about

14 http://www.lloydsbankinggroup.com/media1/economic_insight/halifax_house_price_index_page. asp

retirement. Your government pension is worth nothing,[15] your company or private pension if you have one is tiny, because in 2009–2012 it effectively lost all its value gained in the past 10 years as stock market shares prices tumbled in economic uncertainty and corporate bankruptcies.

You consider selling the house – downsizing – but you will still need to live somewhere, so you buy a smaller house that has also doubled in price over the last 10 years and it costs you £400,000 to buy it. It's okay though because you own your house outright having paid off the mortgage – right?

So after selling and buying (let's not worry about calculating the cost of that right now) you have around £200,000 left to fund your retirement.

How much will you need to budget for a year to cover utility bills, insurance, food, clothes, fun and treats? Use today as a reference... £20,000 per annum or £30,000? How much?

Let's say you can survive on £20,000 a year – you don't eat so much now you are older. You are probably still only 50–65 years, there is plenty of life in you yet – unfortunately. I forgot to ask... how long were you planning to live after you retired? Was it just 10 years? Oh, that's okay then, you can afford that!

If you need more than £20,000 per annum (and you will) or live longer than 10 years – let's hope so – then, to put it politely, you are stuffed. You will have to sell the smaller house you bought to fund your life and it's only a basic life. If you or your partner needs special care, wants a holiday or needs to buy a new car – you can't! Is this the life you planned?

The cold hard fact is that (as things stand now) you cannot get a mortgage again, because either you have already retired or because you only have 5–10 years before you retire and you simply cannot afford the repayments. If you don't sell this smaller property, then you will have to agree to a reversionary mortgage scheme, which releases money from your home to help you afford to live – but the cost is to your family and your legacy.

---

15 http://www.yourpension.org.uk/LPFA/In-The-Scheme/LGPS-Calculator.aspx

These reversionary mortgage schemes are already widely available and most involve you selling your home, your family's inheritance, to an insurance company in return for cash and the right to live there until you die. It's a great way to avoid inheritance tax... you won't have an inheritance to leave! Is this the life you want after 40 years of hard work?

So, who will step in and save you? Not the government – they are broke. Let's hope you have children because they are going to have to buy everything for you.

There is no point even trying to imagine how your children will cope when they want to retire, they will have used up all of their resources to support their ageing parents – that's you. Who will take care of them when, in effect, they have even less? They were born bankrupt[16] and didn't even know it. Each new child starts life owing £17,000 for our overspending, greed and stupidity. Isn't it time we turned that around?

Where we look to our parents to pass down a mortgage-free property to us, our children will have no property of their own as they sold it to pay for your retirement after you sold everything you had!

It doesn't have to be this way. There is another way.

Truth

There is such a thing as 'good debt' – where money is leveraged through bank (or other) lending to buy assets such as property. These assets then make a profit to pay the cost of borrowing and create an income for the investor. It is what I have done and what my clients are doing with me. In Chapter 3, Lesson 3 on page 57, I take the scene I described above and show you how you can fund your retirement and that of your children.

---

16 http://bit.ly/Borne-Bankrupt

Myth 4: if you save for your retirement or have a pension you will be fine

Fact: Pensions are only returning about 3–4% growth if you are lucky; normal savings 1–3%

Even property in London can offer cash returns of 4–7% per annum. If you get smarter about your investment strategy, then some properties easily return over 20% on your cash invested. That means that if you put the same pot of money in a building society account, you could earn (let's be generous) 2%, whereas property would return 20+% and in time there would be capital growth as well.

Do you have a private pension? Have you looked at how much it would pay out on retirement? We looked at Bob's pension to get a sense of what was happening. Apparently, his pension is a high-performing pension with generous employer contributions. Look at these shocking figures:

£150,000 would result in £7,200 per year. That is *either* food *or* heating and light – we couldn't afford both. If I took the lump sum and invested it in property using the simple model below, watch how the returns can grow:

£150,000 using mortgages could buy six properties worth £60,000 each.

Six tenants pay rent and after the mortgage and potential costs are deducted the monthly profit would be 6 x £187.50 – that's £1,125 per month. That's £13,500 per year – already more than the pension would pay out.

Now consider that Bob cannot retire for approximately 25 years (the dates keep moving as people are forced to work for longer) 25 x £13,500 = £337,500.

Now before you get too excited, there are conditions to drawing money from pensions. The money can only be invested in commercial businesses or investments. One financial advisor and pension expert explained to me that to have a reasonable income of £30,000 per year pension you would need to have a pension pot of £1,000,000. I worked out that at the current rate of contributions Bob would need to work for sixty six and half years if we assume that his pension has been accumulating at £15,000 per working year. So never mind the press reports and government legislation, the reality is that without our property investments Bob would not be able to retire until he was 96!

Truth

So, the myth is busted based on the numbers. Most people think they have a pension and that they are all right, but have you checked what your pension might be worth? The second problem many people have experienced is that the majority of pensions are invested in the stock market, which has been steadily underperforming for the last four years. Even your savings are being eaten up by price rises caused by inflation. How long do you want to wait to retire? And what kind of life do you want to live when you do?

Myth 5: there will always be affordable housing

Fact: your children will not be able to afford their own home unless they qualify for a government scheme, if they still exist

The cold hard fact is that we live on a small island with a growing and ageing population that needs somewhere to live. 37% of owned property is under occupied.[17] There is no money, either from the government or from the lenders, to fund the builders to renovate or build new property on the scale that is required. We are suffering from a housing shortage. In 2011, over three million people aged 20–34 years were still living at home.[18]

According to the latest estimates, there are over 930,000[19] empty homes in the UK, with a third of those empty for more than six months. It is clearly a scandal – but also an opportunity.

At the moment, 26.1% of the population (all aged under 40 years) can't afford to own their own homes, and in great swathes of the country house

---

17 English Housing Survey 2009–10 http://www.communities.gov.uk/publications/corporate/ statistics/ehs200910householdreport

18 http://www.telegraph.co.uk/news/uknews/9406877/Census-reveals-housing-shortage.html

19 http://www.emptyhomes.com/statistics-2/

prices are too high.[20] And this is when the housing market is in a slump and prices are low (relatively speaking). What happens when house prices start to rise again? And they will because simple economics states that demand is greater than supply. As soon as banks start lending again the prices will start to rise.

Will wages rise at the same rate?

During 2003–2007, house prices rose by 50%; wages rose by 18%. In the last few years, property prices have fallen and speculation slowed, so both property and wages have seen a 2% increase, but this is on top of already unaffordable purchase prices for the first-time buyer – without whom the market just does not work.[21]

So property prices increase because of supply and demand issues. They also increase because of speculation and other market forces. The opposite is true of wages. Yes, they rise but are limited by the impact on the cost of service or production depending on the sector you work in. Each product or service will have its own supply and demand issues affecting price and that dictates the wages of the workers. So, rather than the item (house) increasing in value because of demand, the item (products or services) needs to generate a profit and so restricts wages.

Houses are an emotional item for most people. They don't need to make a profit. In fact you may even think they are an asset when in fact they are a liability.

Robert Kiyosaki describes assets and liabilities in his book *Rich Dad, Poor Dad*. He states that an asset puts money in your pocket without the need for you to work; a liability takes money from your pocket even when you do work. Your house is a liability; your car is a liability.

---

20 Two reports from the NHPAU, Housing Affordability: A Fuller Picture, and Evaluating Requirements for Market and Affordable Housing – the latter prepared by Professor Steve Wilcox of the University of York and Professor Glen Bramley of Heriot-Watt University – provide a thorough analysis of housing affordability.

21 http://www.lloydsbankinggroup.com/media1/economic_insight/halifax_house_price_index_page.asp

So the bottom line is that more than half of graduates[22] and 26% of people aged under 40 years old can't afford to buy property – this means that they have to live with parents or rent a house. House prices will go up as soon as lending returns to the market or the housing demand pressure builds to exploding point. How are you going to help your children?

Truth

If you understand property as I do, you will recognise this as an opportunity. You can buy property now while the prices are still relatively low. Buy property as an investment vehicle rather than a home chosen with your heart rather than your head. These properties can then be rented out in return for a profit and that income can help you and your children live a more affordable life.

Myth 6: our children believe they can't or simply don't want to invest in property

Fact: property is a great investment that is tangible, in demand and allows you direct control over the amount of income it generates

There are two parts to this myth and both are to do with how some people think. On the one hand, there are people out there who think it 'will all be okay' – the government will take care of them and their children will be fine. They are living in cloud cuckoo land[23] – a fanciful place in their imagination. On the other hand, there are the doomsayers, for example newspaper articles constantly stating how tough things are, and sadly our children are being influenced by them. This book will present solutions and a way to think differently.

I believe the first myth will have shown you that it will not 'all be okay', that the economy in all its complex forms will not sustain our lives built on mounting debt the way it has for the past 50–70 years. If banks still exist and if our children are eligible for loans, then they may need to borrow such

---

22 http://www.dailymail.co.uk/news/article-408816/More-half-graduates-afford-buy-home.html

23 Aristophane's The Birds – http://www.phrases.org.uk/meanings/cloud-cuckoo-land.html

an extraordinary amount of money, which they have no hope of repaying in their lifetime, that property may become a burden that is passed down through generations with grandchildren continuing to pay for property bought by their grandparents.

This makes buying a property sound like a dangerous activity – I believe it is if you do not understand exactly what you are getting into by taking on that debt. If you do not have a plan to repay the debt, then, yes, it is dangerous and foolish.

What about the doomsayers? Are they right? Well, maybe they are for some people following the traditional approach to home ownership. I do not know *you*, the reader, personally, and I do not know your current financial position. What I do know is that we are failing the next generation, our children, and our grandchilden. We are allowing government decisions and our past spending habits to burden them with debt and we are denying them the knowledge and tools to change things. I do not offer financial advice but I am passionate about sharing my financial understanding.

When I work with my clients I ask them to look at a number of resources they have (that we all have):

- How much time do you have? Do you work full time?
- How much cash or equity do you have to invest?
- What is your attitude towards risk versus perceived reward?
- What does your family consist of? How many children and partners, parents or siblings do you have?
- What kind of life are you looking to create for yourself and your family?

The answers to these questions help me to explain what I have accomplished and how it is possible to achieve a different outcome to those outlined in the newspapers. I am not the only one. I have friends and now clients who have achieved the same outstanding results: freedom from a job, funded by a property portfolio that gives us the choice to do what we want and run the businesses we choose.

On page 57, I explain, using examples, how you can take your current assets (cash or equity) and invest in property in a way that helps you to have financial freedom. I also explain in detail how you can help your children to buy their own home or a collection of houses that give them freedom to live where they want and work how they choose. And they won't have to wait until they are 35 years old to achieve it either!

Truth

The truth is that the specific solution will be different for everyone, but the broad principle is the same.

By the end of this book you will be more aware of the financial resources you have access to and you can always go on to read *Using Other People's Money; How to invest in property* to extend this knowledge. By the end of this book you will also think differently about income and assets, the value of money and how to leverage it and therefore just what you need to cover your cost of living.

As you share the lessons in this book, your children will learn about money, debt, assets and liabilities. They will learn lessons not taught in school. They will graduate with a property portfolio that provides a secure baseline of income to enable them to go on a create wonderful lives, possibly discover new medical treatments, technological advances, create works of art or music or become amazing athletes – become whatever they choose because they can. Meanwhile you will be comfortable in your retirement, which perhaps you took early. You will certainly neither be a burden to your children nor reliant on the government for handouts.

Myth 7: listen to your teachers, listen to the government – they know best

Fact: hardly any school teachers are successful property investors, yet most government ministers own two properties – what are you not being told?

Having been a teacher myself at college and university, I know the majority of teachers do an amazing job. The problem with education is that it is out of date for the modern world and shackled by government legislation and targets.

If you want to be a successful athlete, for example a runner, who would you watch or want to train with? If you want to be a racing driver, who would you want to teach you? If you want to know about the universe, whose books would you read? If you want to know how to make money and be successful in business or property investment, would you ask a teacher?

We are bound and limited by the people around us, their experiences, their beliefs and their ideas. So does this mean that if we mix with inspirational and successful people, we will be inspired and become successful? I believe so.

Think about the people you mix with and the conversations you have. Are your conversations about your collective worries about money? Do you talk about what you lack and do not have enough of? Are your conversations predominantly negative?

Think what this does to your mind? If all you talk about is negative, then your unconscious mind will filter the information (the millions of gigabytes of information every day) to look out for information that reinforces your beliefs.

Look around the room or the train or wherever you are reading this book. You have 30 seconds to count how many blue objects you can see. Now close your eyes and tell me how many red things you saw? You can't because you were focused on the blue. Yet, the red things are there too if you look for them.

What about a different type of conversation: the drama of other people's lives? This includes listening to the news, reading magazines full of stories of so-called celebrities (who they are dating, divorcing, etc.) What do you watch on television? Now, just to be clear, I like television. I watch dramas and crime programmes for entertainment, but I don't watch programmes that revel in the misery of others. I don't have to watch them to be part of the conversation with my friends.

Then there are the conversations where you take ideas and grow them; you explore new learning or share insights. Personally, I enjoy watching debates and discussions on the economy. I like to talk about developments in business and thinking. I like to talk about property deals.

I can also have fun and relax – I am not too boring to go out with. I just don't want to spend my time discussing what happened during a miserable television show, the latest tragedy involving a child or the latest political or celebrity scandal. Fortunately, neither do my friends. Every one of them is fascinating and fun and I enjoy their company and learn something new every day.

Truth

I have learnt more about life since I left school and used my new knowledge more effectively than when solving any maths equation. Don't misunderstand me; I totally agree that we need to learn the basic skills of maths and English. However, even though I have two degrees and taught at University for years, I am not convinced that a business degree is worth three years of anyone's life, never mind £30,000 of debt!

Work out what you want in life and then look for (research if you need to) people who are successfully living the life you would like to move towards. Work out what they have done, read their books, listen to them speak. Take a chance to work with them if you can. It's called 'modelling'. Get better and more relevant teachers.

Summary

If the seven myths have done anything, I hope that they have helped you to see that you need to think differently.

- Do you still think the government can support you in a retirement you would like?
- Do you think buying a family home will give you future security?
- Do you think paying off your personal mortgage is your current number one priority?
- Do you think your children will be able to afford their own home?
- Do you think your children want your home (if you haven't sold it by then)?
- Do you think traditional education is keeping up with the pace of technology and is teaching your children how it will impact on the way future generations live their lives?
- Are schools and the government explaining to your children (or you) how they plan to tackle the burgeoning economic debt?
- Do you think future increases in property prices will solve the economic crisis and your financial future?
- Do you trust the media, the government, the banks or your faith in the future?
- Do you think your children have the financial education they need?

If you answered no to the majority of the questions above, then please read on. If you answered yes, then please go back and re-read the myths. Follow the links, do your research and please come to your own conclusion. If you then decide to do nothing, at least you can't blame anyone for not telling you how bad things were or that you needed to change the way you were thinking. A fundamental understanding of how money works is crucial because you are the head of your own family business, whether or not you realise it.

Chapter 3 looks at the seven lessons you and your children were not taught in school and how understanding them will change your life.

Chapter 3

The seven most important financial lessons you will ever learn

I want to turn education and popular belief on its head so that you can share your understanding with your children and teach them what education is failing to tell them. I want to help you and your family make decisions about your lives and property investment in a way that better suits how your children will interact with property. I want to help your family prepare for, and thrive through, the coming economic and financial storm.

I have made an assumption that you do want to provide for your family's financial future, otherwise you might not be reading this book. I want to make it clear that by understanding this new way of thinking about money, property and the coming shift in our economic future, you will also be preparing for your own financial future should you become redundant, want early retirement or to move into business.

You could work through this chapter together with your family. Listening to your younger children – discussing what is important to them gives you an incredible insight into parts of them you might not have recognised. Children as young as four or five are already stating that caring for the environment is important.

We all go to school, theoretically, to get a good education. In fact, we are trained in the small sphere that government believes is important to us. What they are repeatedly missing is that the pace of knowledge and understanding is multiplying to the Nth degree. Our children get this, but the teachers and politicians of older generations don't. The term 'education' comes from the Latin word meaning to 'pull out' or 'draw out'. Do you feel that your internal knowledge was pulled out of you at school; that it flowed from you?

Ask your children what they think – they are probably bored both with the content and the delivery mechanisms. They may not see the relevance of reciting the alphabet and times tables – you can help! The British education system is not preparing our children for life or the world of work. Young people are not taught about assets and liabilities, about income and expenses in a practical and tangible way.

This book will give you the tools to start your own financial revolution and break your dependence on the state system, while contributing to the lives of your family, future generations and all the families and people that you house in decent homes.

You may have noticed that you do everything online – your access to information and the power to process it – is phenomenal. Education is a limiting factor with its rules about spelling and grammar, individual work, even maths and languages. As a former university lecturer, I honestly believe that we need to help the younger generation identify what they need to learn, point out how easily they can learn it and what its benefits are and then let them get on with it – because they are quicker and have access to more information than we ever had.

The greatest gifts you can give your children are, first, the game of Monopoly™, then move on to the board game CashFlow™ and buy Robert Kiyosaki's books for children. They were, after all, born to keep you in the style you would like your old age to be – luxurious. So you'd better give your children the education to manage their money and ensure they invest it wisely in property and not the building society or designer clothes!

The wealthy don't work for money – they make money work for them and some people are better at doing this than others. Obvious examples of people who have mastered this skill are traditional business owners, big corporations and, of course, people like Lord Alan Sugar, Sir Richard Branson and hundreds of other well-known people. There are also thousands of smaller businesses run by successful business owners living great lives that they determine and control.

There are also people employed by businesses who love their jobs. They, too, have sold something they have – time – in return for money. Or maybe the satisfaction of a job well done, companionship or status. Even employees are small businesses, they just don't realise it.

So what are the seven most important lessons that you never learnt in school? Again, I am assuming you didn't take an accounting or economics degree, but even if you did I may still challenge the status quo of traditional thinking.

In this chapter I am going to cover the following:

1. Lenders and how to get on their good side – a brief and simple history of banking and the money markets
2. Why money must keep moving
3. Leverage – making your money work for you
4. Why your savings are not worth a penny
5. Build a portfolio now
6. Letting go of old habits
7. Who is in your team?

In school, we are taught about currencies and denominations – not the history of the creation of money, how to use it and the alternatives. I am not going to delve too far into the future shape and use of money, but just far enough to shock you. Let's start with understanding the lenders and how we got to be in the mess we are in…

Lesson 1: lenders and how to get on their good side – a brief and simple history of banking and the money markets

I want to explain a little about commercial lending from my perspective and experience, and more about finance and lending in general. In 2009, I needed to understand how 'money worked', so that when I approached my high-street bank to see whether I could borrow money from them to invest in property I could understand their business; what they needed from an ideal client. Moving to more commercial lending meant having conversations as a business client of the bank, which entails a whole different language. It also sparked an interest in the whole system way beyond my previous understanding. I am not an expert, simply a keen student.

Without going back to historic times, money has been around the globe for thousands of years. It started with the use of shells and the like as a means to trade unwanted or excess goods, produce and services with another person or community.

Banks become a more formal institution as a place to store the gold that replaced shells (and other artefacts) as the preferred method of exchange. Paper money was initially a note that confirmed you had gold deposited in one store and it was easier to trade the paper note than the gold itself. That all sounds sensible, but then of course there is always more...

Skip forward and the original gold deposit-style of banks was surpassed by private banks that started to print notes and lend them privately. In 1694, during the reign of King William III and Queen Mary II, the Bank of England was established as the central bank of England designed to act on behalf of the government during war with France.[24] It was to be nationalised in 1946 after the Second World War. It's strange how wars and money are always so inextricably linked!

The creation of paper money and the rise of the private banks were causing chaos as the value of the notes bore no real or tangible worth and was responsible for repeating cycles of inflation. In 1844, The Bank Charter Act[25] meant that only the Bank of England could issue new legal tender in the form of notes and coins. Their aim was to control inflation and regulate the money supply through its link to reserves of gold. In effect, the rule was the bank could only print money for which it held an equivalent amount of gold *unless* there was a crisis, in which case they could change the rules!

Broadly speaking, there was an emergence of two sorts of banks. First, consumer banks that collected savings deposits from, and lent to, ordinary

---

24 http://en.wikipedia.org/wiki/Bank_of_England http://en.wikipedia.org/wiki/William_III_of_ England#War_in_Europe

25 http://en.wikipedia.org/wiki/Bank_Charter_Act_1844

people. These banks relied on and served people who worked and accumulated personal surplus cash, which they then deposited in the bank for safekeeping. This money was lent to other people for a fee. It was tangible real money and the bank only lent what it had. Second, there were investment banks, which were the accumulated wealth of a specific number of business partners who pooled their money and lent it to bigger projects and to businesses. Investment banks evaluated the risks carefully as they were lending their own money, however this was still considered a more speculative form of lending with higher risks and rewards.

Financial innovation and the invention of derivatives flowed smoothly into the markets as the volume of lending exploded across the globe. Subprime mortgage lending in America quadrupled between 2000 and 2006 – we have all heard of the phrase NINJA (no income, no job or assets) mortgages. In fact, this is all debt and is one of the reasons why Iceland went bankrupt, Greece is bankrupt in all but name and Spain, Ireland, Portugal and Italy all teeter on the brink of the fiery pit.

The point of this chapter is to explain how we moved from a system of trade which had a value attached to a system of creating pretend money that has no value which is lent to other people (us) for a fee (interest). The interest then comes back into the central pot and is lent out again.

The problem is that we are both borrowing and lending more than we have, which makes the money worthless. Also, we are borrowing and lending it to people and countries that cannot afford to pay the interest due. This means that the money is flowing in one direction and that is a very dangerous position for a system built on the flow of money (debt) and the payment of fees (interest).

To understand more about this history, and particularly the recent recessions and immediate causes and effects, you can read the papers and books produced by Raghuram Rajan, Eliot Spitzer, Satyajit Das and Charles Morris. For an easier, jargon-free read about why our financial system is doomed, read Simon Dixon (see the Bibliography on page 103).

So why have I written so much about the banking system? Because our confidence and, therefore, our futures are linked to what happens across the globe now. The economy of one country affects all, as the complex web of loans and debts ensnares all who pass by, including you just minding your own business.

Ironically, in the section about credit cards on page 43 you will see how the general public has repeated the errors of governments and countries in their approach to borrowing, which is why so many people are struggling in debt and crisis like mini human Greeces.

You may have heard the comment that trillions of pounds are circulating around the globe at any one time. It is, but as digital debt – not real promissory notes backed up by tangible gold deposits. The problem is that instead of always lending real tangible money or paper notes backed by gold deposits held in vaults, banks now lend 4, 10 or 40 times the actual money they have to back them up. In recent years, you may have noticed that your credit card limits or bank overdrafts have been reduced without warning. This is because lenders will have technically promised you, in advance, that you can use that money if you need it. Now they need it; they want to lend it to other people for a fee, not have it sitting there 'just in case' you might want it!

What does the future hold? More of the same, sadly! No matter what Europe proposes in terms of regulation, America with its powerfully placed advocates of high-risk (high-reward and consequences be damned) lending will never agree. Obama, with the 'mandate for change', appointed the leaders of the original banking system that created this crisis to positions of power designed to change the current system. What do you think is going to happen?

Simon Dixon advocates that a dramatic change is needed – that we must regulate the production of money and reduce our reliance on debt. I agree. I believe that with greater knowledge comes greater power. By the end of this chapter, in just 27 pages, you will understand more about money and how it works so that you can make it work for you, using the current debt-driven system to acquire income generation assets.

We need to start the money moving at the bottom of the food chain again; we need to get spending personally and commercially, in a responsible, debt-free way that is calculated to promote business and commerce. We need to go around the outside of these major banks and investment houses to the private individuals with money. These people have also been failed by a system designed to support the 'uber-rich' on a scale that we cannot even comprehend.

So what about using credit cards as a financial tool?

Since I started to research money and how it works, I realised that I could both use the system to my own advantage – for the benefit of my family – and work round the system.

By understanding concepts like return on investment (ROI) and leverage (see Lesson 3 on page 56), I understand more about debt. I recognise the system is broken, but I can also borrow money – make it work for me – so I can do other things. I can make sure that my money earns enough to pay the interest that I owe and I can keep the profit as, in effect, my wage.

I can then also work outside the system and work with private money (non-banking, tangible non-debt cash). I can help others to leverage their assets and I can use my surplus cash to fund other projects.

Like all lending, the most important thing before you start is to understand how much it is going to cost you to borrow the money, when you can pay it back and who is going to pay the interest in the meantime. The biggest risk with borrowing money is the variable nature of the interest rate. This can be managed by either borrowing the money at an agreed fixed cost upfront or by developing systems to manage the risk – through monitoring and spreading it across your investment portfolio. I use a mixture of all of the above.

There is one other factor I would like to mention and that is the actual cost of borrowing in general – so much of the media is focused on the notional Bank of England base rate and how it is at an all-time low and set to stay low, with latest predictions saying three years plus before it starts to rise.

What the press is not reporting loudly is that the mortgage companies borrow their money against something called LIBOR (London Interbank Offered Rate[26]). This is currently averaging about 1% and climbing. Ironically, even LIBOR is at the centre of a political and ethical debate. Whether or not this method of monitoring inter-bank lending confidence has to be replaced, remains to be seen.

In late 2011, Mervin King the governor of the Bank of England warned[27] that mortgage rates (and borrowing costs) would rise as lenders passed on the cost of their borrowing to their customer. In May 2012, Halifax and associated lenders increased[28] their Standard Variable Rate (SVR), affecting millions of borrowers who thought they were secure!

While this is tangential to the understanding of credit cards, I believe it serves as a great lesson in understanding the risk involved in borrowing money. However, there are also rewards if you 'play your cards right!' In its simplest form, a credit card if used properly can give you up to 45 days extra money – interest free. In its most strategic form, it can lend you most of the deposit or costs for a property investment project at 0% interest for between 9 and 15 months! Your challenge, with everything associated to borrowing money, is to understand the money flow of your deal. When you will pay it back, where that money will come from, and who is going to pay the interest on the money while the project is being worked.

The next challenge is how to borrow money on a credit card without affecting your credit score. Please be aware that lenders share financial information about you behind the scenes as they are all owned by one massive shareholder – us, through the government.

Banks want you to stay ignorant of the game and how it works. On the one hand, they want you to take out credit cards and buy stuff that really you can't afford, so that at the end of the month you can't clear your credit card balance and instead pay them an extortionate rate of interest

26 http://en.wikipedia.org/wiki/Libor

27 http://www.thisismoney.co.uk/money/mortgageshome/article-2068973/Sir-Mervyn-King-warns-mortgage-rates-likely-soar-tells-banks-slash-bonuses.html

28 http://news.sky.com/home/business/article/16219481

because we are a debt-fuelled economy, as already discussed. On the other hand, they now also want you to be a perfect borrower. From a secured lending perspective, the underwriters of loans and mortgages need you to demonstrate that you know how to manage your money. The way that you can do this is to limit the amount of unsecured borrowing (credit cards) that you have available, clear your balances regularly, yet keep borrowing and paying back.

What you must understand is how a lender views the activity on your credit record and how this affects your credit score and, ultimately, your ability to borrow money through mortgages:

- First, do not apply for too many credit cards at once or apply to have your existing cards increase their limits. Just by asking, you are affecting your credit score whether or not you are successful.

- Second, when you have cards, do not 'max them out' and use every last pound available to you, as you will look out of control and desperate for cash. Have a strategy to pay back your cards regularly and even overpay them now and then.

Credit cards are a brilliant tool for business owners and property investors; they act as a free overdraft and ease cashflow. They can also be leveraged by enabling you to buy stock and sell it for a profit before the interest or loan becomes repayable. In the dynamic financial climate we find ourselves in it is difficult to write any clear, hard and fast rules other than know what you are doing! I have produced an ebook on credit cards. Go to: www. TheSourcersApprentice.com and download it from the resource section.

Credit scores – crucial to your financial future

Credit scores are a system of measuring your predicted ability to repay a borrowed debt. If you intend to make your money work for you and leverage your assets, then borrowing money from somewhere is inevitable. Let's focus on the banks to start with and then move on to private lenders.

In the personal lending market (including small businesses), there are two primary agencies called Equifax and Experian. They keep records on you, which you are entitled to review (and challenge if necessary). This includes personal data such as where you live, whether you are registered to vote and a list of your financial associations. Financial associations mean anyone with whom you entered into a joint financial commitment – this could be a personal loan, though more typically it would be a bank account or a mortgage. Now the person you are linked to influences how the lenders see your score. During a divorce, this is how one partner is negatively impacted by the poor financial behaviour of the other partner, and this financial mud sticks. Next, comes a list of the loans or credit you have access to, for example mortgages, personal loans, car loans and credit cards.

I noticed in the last year or so that my daughter has been receiving unsolicited post offering her a credit card at ridiculous interest rates of over 30–40%. So many young people will be tempted by this seemingly easy cash that they will not realise the true cost of the shoes or jumper they have bought until it is too late.

All our children have mobile, internet-active devices along with their assorted contracts. The taking out of one of these contracts will have initiated a credit search and an entry on their credit report. If they miss a payment (even one), their future credit history is damaged for up to a year or more. Just £30 can ruin a credit score! Missing payments is perceived as the first step to financial problems, either through lack of management and organisation or through lack of funds and over commitment. Either way, it is frowned upon and penalised.

Gearing is another measure that a lender uses to gauge your suitability for borrowing. This is based on how much you have actually borrowed, particularly on unsecured lending like credit cards, against how much available credit you have. If you are highly geared, for example you have one card and it is near to its credit limit, then a lender may view you as living beyond your means, meaning that you could be at risk of defaulting.

You need to get to a position where you are borrowing under 50% of your potential borrowing, and so have a gearing ratio of less than 50%. How do you work this out? Add up the total debt on all your credit cards and divide it by the total of all your credit limits.

I have guessed the figure of 50%. When I first increased my credit cards to cover my property training costs, my credit rating dropped through the floor. I called the credit agencies and spoke with them – they can be very helpful. They explained about gearing and I started to experiment by paying off my 0% credit cards bit by bit as they came to the end of the life of the offers. I noticed that my credit rating started to improve as my gearing ratio moved towards 60%. Of course, other factors will have been at play, such as the number of searches on my record, but I do believe gearing is now a significant decision-making factor.

So the trick to managing your credit score is similar to managing your credit cards:

1. Know what you are doing and keep a record.
2. Keep your overall borrowing low relative to the amount you could borrow.
3. Again, set up direct payments for the minimum amount to avoid missed payments and make sure you have the funds to pay.

I would also say think about how your lending looks to an agency whose job it is to score you. Do you look like a risk? Are you constantly applying for loans and credit cards? Think carefully and manage wisely for as long as you want to borrow from the establishment!

Of course, you could borrow funds from family, friends or a private investor – how would they check you out? Well, they could ask you to provide your credit score or they could just check you out online. That is going to be how decisions are made in future. Your children uploading 'inappropriate' party photos with friends will find their history remains on the web forever. Future employers, business partners, lenders and friends will be able to trace your history and that of your children long after you have forgotten about a photo. Do you check what pictures your children or friends upload of you?

I remember a photo of one friend (who appeared on the television programme *Secret Millionaire*) who had been tagged in a late night compromising position appearing on my Facebook page. A quick email and the picture was untagged and the perpetrator unfriended, but what if I had not noticed? Are you checking your social profile?

If you are active online, you might have a PeerIndex score or a Klout Score, maybe a Kred Score or Ecademy ranking. How many friends and connections do you have? How many blogs do you post? How many videos do you upload? How often do you interact with others online – sharing news and information – engaging in a debate?

Once again, the point here is that time and technology are changing at an extraordinary rate and we need to keep aware and keep up! With a growing distrust of everyone, government and banking, lenders will need to qualify people who are suitable as potential borrowers. Maybe your social media score will more accurately indicate how successful you are likely to be than an arbitrary credit score. After all, true wealth is what you have that enables you to create wealth all over again once it is lost.

Interest and how your spending habits will send you broke

There are two final sub-lessons under this heading. First, how interest is often forgotten in the rush and passion of a purchase, which can result in the bargain costing more, much more, than originally perceived! Second, spending cash from your capital pot, especially if it is not an income-generating asset, is actually madness.

Lesson 1 is about how money works; it is about interest and about credit cards. If your children do not know and understand how money works, then they are not only risking their credit scores they are actually throwing away their hard-earned cash!

A purchase made on a credit card that is not paid off in the 'free' period actually accrues interest at a rate of at least 20% in most cases. Just borrow £5,000 and fail to clear the debt on an interest-accruing credit card and watch as £80 plus is added to your next statement.

This does not mean that credit cards or loans are bad or something to be feared – it means they are tools that need to be mastered. An advanced lesson is to recognise the cost of borrowing and that what appears to be an opportunity or a bargain can actually cost a lot more when interest, fees and costs are included.

The only time a debt should remain uncleared past the due date on a credit card is when the interest rate is 0% and the purchase was related to an income-generating purchase. Without getting too preachy, the main problem with the debt many people are suffering today is that they bought items, often 'luxury' items, without considering how they were going to make the repayments.

This brings us to simple home accounts and budgeting. Having brought up two teenagers myself, and knowing how difficult it was at times to communicate with them, you may think I am mad to make this next suggestion. The important fact is that you can empower your children to understand about money, its value and how it can be leveraged by encouraging them to plan and monitor their expenses and savings for specific purchases. Maybe this involves using an Excel spreadsheet of their monthly expenditure. In fact, maybe you need that for your own household expenses. (Go to www.TheSourcersApprentice.com resources.)

If you understand the benefit and advantages of keeping an account of your expenses and see it either as a game or a challenge, then it can be easier to motivate yourself. I had to keep a record of my spending when I was a single parent and really struggling on very little money. I learnt that if I managed my money really well, then I could actually get the bank to give me more money than I deposited – that extra £60–80 per annum made a real difference to how we spent our summer holidays!

When my older daughter, Kimberley decided that she wanted to buy her own home and I explained how mortgages are calculated (but, more importantly, the reality of how, as a future homeowner, you need to know that you can afford the repayments), she soon created a spreadsheet to help her understand how she spent her money and to see what was left each month. She noted how much she could save and what things she was spending on. That led her to reduce spending in certain areas of her life – or think twice about a purchase – so that she could reach her goal more quickly.

When Charlie, my younger daughter wanted to go travelling to South Africa I explained how Excel worked and she drew up a spreadsheet to list all the expenses expected on her trip – her globetrotting budget. Then, she worked out how much she could earn and how long it would take her to save her budget. Within nine months she had saved her budget, flights were booked and she was walking through the departure gates at Terminal Five. She mastered budgeting so well that she extended a three-month trip to six months.

What do your children want or think they want to have or experience? By the end of this book you will be able to show them how investing in property will help them to have everything they want and more besides! The passive income and greater return on their cash invested will help them to achieve their goals much sooner than planned. Best of all, they can then spend from the passively earned income and retain their capital invested to generate more income the next month, and then the next month and the next month.

The point here is to understand the difference between paying hidden interest on purchases made through credit cards or loans and actually earning interest from investments that means you can spend for free. If the money earned is not spent, then it can actually start to multiply at a phenomenal rate.

This brings me to the impact of compounding interest. I have created two simple tables to explain my point. In Table 1, I have taken a one pound coin as an example and doubled it every day for 21 days...

Day	£ compounded
1	1
2	2
3	4
4	8
5	16
6	32
7	64
8	128
9	256
10	512
11	1,024
12	2,048
13	4,096
14	8,192
15	16,384
16	32,768
17	65,536
18	131,072
19	262,144
20	524,288
21	1,048,576

Table 1: the powerful effect of compounding

In the early stages of the experiment, nothing much happens as £1 becomes £2 and £8 becomes £16, but look where momentum starts to build at day 13 where £2,048 becomes £4,096 and then again at day 18 where £65,536 becomes £131,072.

Within 21 imaginary days, where you can double your money daily, £1 quickly becomes £1,000,000+.

Now consider Table 2 where you spend money on coffees instead of compounding the benefit…

Day	£ spent	£ accumulated and compounded
1	2.75	5.5
2	2.75	13.75
3	2.75	30.25
4	2.75	63.25
5	2.75	129.25
6	2.75	261.25
7	2.75	525.25
8	2.75	1,053.25
9	2.75	2,109.25
10	2.75	4,221.25
11	2.75	8,445.25
12	2.75	16,893.25
13	2.75	33,789.25
14	2.75	67,581.25
15	2.75	135,165.25
16	2.75	270,333.25
17	2.75	540,669.25
18	2.75	1,081,341.25
19	2.75	2,162,685.25
20	2.75	4,325,373.25
21	2.75	8,650,749.25

Table 2: assume a daily coffee costs £2.75. In 21 days, you would have spent £57.75

If you look at the coffee costs over 21 days, they are approximately £57.75. However, if instead of spending the money on coffee you actually saved it, and used the compounding process shown in Table 1, how much would you accumulate? Each day, your money would double and what you did not spend on coffee would be added to the pot as well. Hopefully, this makes you think about every penny you spend. It certainly changed my spending habits – I mean, really, how many pairs of shoes or necklaces does one girl need? Don't answer that! When you spend money it's gone. When you invest it and make it work for you, you can ultimately spend considerably more!

The bottom line is that banks have lost lots of money in the past and they now need to make a profit. Some have a massive business debt to repay the taxpayer! When you take out a loan consider the cost of any lender fees alongside your interest rate and the term of the tie-in period of the loan. This is obvious when you are dealing with mortgages, but can also apply to loans and even 0% credit cards.

Lesson 2: why money must keep moving

If you do not understand how money moves and what it costs, how can you access it, afford to pay to borrow it and ultimately make it work for you? What are your thoughts about money? Underlying this question is the concept of abundance. This can apply to so many areas of your life. I know without a shadow of a doubt that you are one of the top 10% richest people in the world – simply because you are reading this book. Do you feel abundant? It depends what you use as a comparison, of course. The truth is you are rich in so many ways.

Let's think about water. Is water abundant? You know where to find it and how to gather it when you need to use it, mostly because we are spoilt by taps and Perrier. Yet, if you were about to cross the desert, would you learn even more about water – that precious life-preserving resource? That is what money is – a precious resource. You need to learn about where to find it, how and when to use it, the difference it makes when invested well, the damage it can do when created en-mass and its indirect impact on our planet through war, and all that comes with that.

In brutal terms, if money is really just debt that is actually costing you money (stay with me here), then you need to make it work (or you need to work) to pay back for the pleasure of having it. If you spend it, then not only do you no longer have it but you still owe someone else for it!

It may seem that the only 'real' money you have is the money that you work for. Here, you have definitely given something of value (your time) in exchange. What you don't know – nor do I – is whether your employer has had to borrow money in order to pay you.

Regardless of whether or not you have any 'real' money, I suspect that very few people will be able to live within their means as our parents would have said. Most people will have debt in some form: their home mortgage, a car loan, outstanding credit card balance or a personal loan, possibly something bought on credit like furniture.

That debt will be costing you and in Lesson 1 on page 43 I explained how to convert that debt from a cost to an asset.

Let's stick with this second lesson and the need to make money move. If it sits still in your house as equity, for example, then it is actually shrinking in today's economy. Why? Inflation at the time of writing is averaging 4%.[29] The Halifax reported that house prices fell by 2.4% in April 2012 and that the average house price was £159,883 having fallen for the fourth consecutive month – that is the same price as in August 2004.[30] Even when prices are reported to rise, the rise is small and not guaranteed to last.

What does this mean to you? First, the value of your house is falling. Second, even if it stayed the same it is decreasing in value when inflation is factored into the equation. And, third, have you considered why you are holding on to it? So many people see a debt-free house as a form of security. I do understand – I thought that too until I realised that my house would never feed or clothe me!

---

29 http://www.bankofengland.co.uk/Pages/home.aspx

30 http://www.thisismoney.co.uk/money/mortgageshome/article-1671748/House-prices-What-expect--news-predictions.html

Keeping your money working for you is essential – not just now in a recession that may well last in real terms for the next 4–6 years before we see a return to growth, but also as a way to supplement your income in your old age.

While you might not like the idea of increasing your debt, remember there is a difference between good debt and bad debt. As long as you invest any borrowed money into assets that generate a profit, then you can actually use debt to create money.

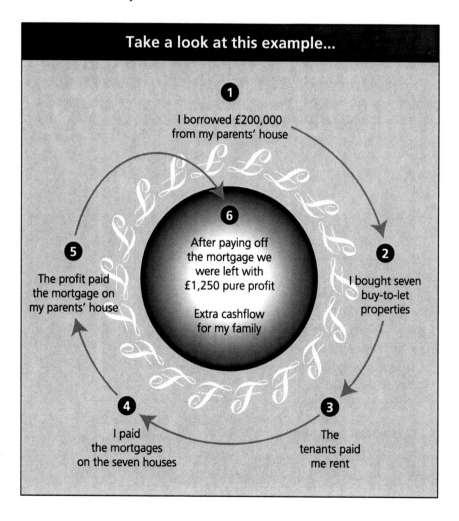

Take a look at this example...

1 I borrowed £200,000 from my parents' house

2 I bought seven buy-to-let properties

3 The tenants paid me rent

4 I paid the mortgages on the seven houses

5 The profit paid the mortgage on my parents' house

6 After paying off the mortgage we were left with £1,250 pure profit

Extra cashflow for my family

As the money moves around the circle other people benefit:

1. As I took out the loan, members of staff were employed to manage the transaction and a broker received a fee.

2. When the houses were bought, solicitors and surveyors were paid. Builders carried out repairs and refurbishments.

3. When the tenants moved in, insurance was taken out, fees were paid, members of staff were employed. Then the letting agency received a fee for managing the property. The tenant moved in to a safe and decent home for their family.

4. As the rent paid first the smaller mortgages and then the main £200,000 loan, bank staff transferred and recorded money – creating more jobs.

5. The profit then moved into our bank account where it increased our monthly cashflow.

In the background, we employ a book keeper and a financial director. We pay for internet access and telephones. We drive cars and buy petrol. Our money fuels the economy and keeps people in work, as well as providing decent homes.

All this movement of money was fuelled by the original loan from the bank. Everyone in the chain has been paid and we still make a profit. Above all, it cost us nothing as all costs were paid for using the money originally borrowed.

We actually got money for nothing. Well, that's not true: I worked out how to do this; I took a calculated risk; I used my time and my knowledge to make it happen. The result though is long-term ongoing cashflow based on one day per month's work.

Lesson 3: leverage – making your money work for you

Leverage is the process of taking an asset and by applying a multiplier you can enhance the performance and outcome of the original asset. By choosing property investment as my tool I can leverage my money.

If, for example, I wanted to buy a house for £100,000 and I had that much in cash, I could buy the property outright. However, I could also get a loan from a bank (mortgage) for £75,000 according to current 'buy-to-let' lending conditions.

Let's ignore costs for the moment. In the first outright purchase, I would receive all the rent (ignore insurance and letting agent fees for a minute). Let's say the rent was £500 per month or £6,000 per year. In the second theoretical example, I could buy four properties at £100,000 each using a mortgage of £75,000 and a £25,000 deposit on each one.

If I bought the four houses using four mortgages, I would obviously need to repay a monthly mortgage cost. This might be in the region of £75,000 at 5%/12 = £312.50 per month per property. Each month I would make £187.50 profit on each property, totalling £750 per month and £9,000 per year – in effect returning 150% more money each year than by owning just one property outright.

This is the power of leverage: splitting an investment and using other people's money, for a sensible fee, to increase the return on your investment – everyone wins. This is how I became financially free in under two years and published my first book called *Using Other People's Money: How to Invest in Property*.

So, if everything that you think of as money is actually debt, then it has to work to grow to beat the cost of inflation. When market conditions actually change you can then watch as the rising prices reduce your debt and heighten your leverage even further. Look at this next example:

If we buy a £100,000 house using a mortgage of £75,000, the debt is £75,000. Buy-to-let mortgages are agreed on an interest-only basis. The debt is not reduced during the period of the loan as all the monthly payments are used to pay back the interest costs and none of the capital borrowed as in a residential (capital and interest) mortgage. So in 10 years' time, even 20 years, you will still owe the bank £75,000!

If you look at house prices since records began, you can see that house prices have doubled on average every seven to ten years. So what if we assume that it might take 10 years until the value of a property is worth double today's price? That means that in 2023 the £100,000 house would be worth £200,000. The question is how much is the debt?

The answer is £75,000!!

This means that if you used leverage and bought four houses priced £100,000 each over the next 12 months and waited 10 years, you would have a property portfolio of £800,000 with only £300,000 of debt – that is a massive half a million pounds for doing nothing, *plus* you will have been receiving over £9,000[31] a year in rental income.

Bear in mind that this is an example to prove a point. I have missed out some of the costs to buy and I have missed out the management costs needed to ensure your portfolio is a high-performing asset, but I am sure you will agree that the principle is very exciting.

---

31 All these figures are approximate to make the example easy, but they are based on my experience of house prices and rental income.

Imagine you made this investment for your eight-year-old child. They would then have all the income they needed to attend university. In fact, you could have paid for their private school education as well.

Imagine you helped your 18 or 20-year-old child to do this. As a family, you would have considerable income from the portfolio – enough to pay the rent for your child to live where they choose, enough to pay for you to live where you choose (as you also leave home and turn your empty nest into a property shared by professional tenants for yet more income).

Leverage has been applied to money to show how it works mathematically. It can also be applied to time. Whether you have a job or a business you will be exchanging your time for money: profit or wages. Again, using property you can buy a portfolio and then work less than one day per month (it depends on the size of your portfolio and the strategy you have used) to monitor it. You will have a team of letting agents and builders if you need them.

The property will then generate your monthly profit over and over again – all for just one day's work per month. So using the example above again, you could earn £750 for just a few hours' work (as that is all that would be needed for four properties, maybe even just one hour a month).

The property itself and the team around you become the leveraging tool. That is why my busy clients use me to find, fix and fill their property portfolio – in part because I have the knowledge and experience, but also to use (leverage) my time to save theirs.

So while your home is not an asset and money needs to be kept moving to make money, you can also use other people's time to create the portfolio and, in doing so, turn your home from a liability to an investment tool.

Lesson 4: why your savings are not worth a penny

In Chapter 2, myth 3 (see page 24) I explained that your home as a future nest egg was a fallacy. Now I will take the lesson one step further and explain why your savings are not worth a penny and how you can make them work for you.

I will only touch on the fact that your money is not that safe in a bank briefly. Here are the reasons why:

- A run on the banks (as we saw with Northern Rock) will mean that you cannot access the notes if the bank cannot dispense them – you are not in control. NatWest customers experienced this in 2012 because of a computer glitch.
- If inflation spirals, then using a wheelbarrow to move your money around is just impractical, but it is an approach used in some developing and so-called developed countries.[32]
- You are only getting 1–3% on your savings with inflation at 4+%. This means your savings are shrinking the longer they stay in the bank!

How can you tell what investment makes sense? What are the pros and cons of the stock market and other investment classes? ROI or cash-on-cash return gives you a tangible equation to compare different investments based on the net return (or profit) that you get on an annual basis for each sum invested.

The formula is simple:

- Above the dividing line is the net profit from the investment. So, in the example of buying a buy-to-let property, above the line is the annual net rent. This is the gross rent from the tenant minus the letting agent fees, the mortgage and the property insurance. This could be the interest earned on savings or other investment income.
- Below the dividing line are all the cash costs needed to get the property to a point where it produces rent. Therefore, the deposit on the property, the solicitor, surveyor and broker fees, costs to refurbish the property, gas certificates, tenant search fees and, when sourcing for a bespoke client, my sourcing fee. This could be the cost of investing cash into a deal.

When you divide the smaller top number by the larger bottom number you will get a figure less than one. Maybe 0.10 or anything from 0.04–0.35 – this is effectively a percentage (10, 4 or 35%). This means that this investment would earn you that percentage income, and so you can compare that to the

---

32 http://www.cato.org/zimbabwe

potentially less risky investment offered by using savings accounts and the interest you earn.

You can use this information to calculate potential profit shares in a business, investments in anything from shares, gold to property. This is a more comparable measure to calculate the difference between two investment opportunities as it includes all costs, rather than yield which some investors use – especially in the property world – as this is a broad, gross figure.

I hope that you can now see that not only do you need to change the way you think about property, you also need to question how to get the best return on your savings.

Lesson 5: build a property portfolio now

You now understand leverage and how to apply that to your resources. You also know what it means to understand the return on your time invested. This is the cornerstone of leverage: how and where can you grow your money?

I have also briefly hinted that you can spend, save or invest and that when you invest there are different asset classes – things you can invest in and that they have different levels of control over them. Let's look at the asset classes in slightly more detail and then I will explain ROI or return on investment (cash invested) as a way to compare how efficiently you are using your money.

There are five asset classes:

- Commodities.
- Stocks and shares.
- Business.
- Precious metals.
- Property.

Commodities are the output products of businesses that can be traded, such as oil, electricity, other fuels, food and drink (for example wine, coffee or corn) and minerals, for example metals. Mostly bought through a broker, you effectively buy a share of a product and gamble that, as it is traded around the world on the commodities market, demand for this primary or raw product rises and so does your profit.

Stocks and shares in their simplest form are where you give some money in exchange for a percentage of the future profit of a company you like. You can't influence any of the decisions the company makes about its business practices, you are a passive observer of the performance.

Business is straightforward. You can invest your money in your own business, you can invite others to join you and you can share the profit when you make it. If this is your own business, then you have control over the decisions and the profits, but you will need to invest your time alongside your money to see the best returns.

Precious metals are relatively simple to understand. Here, you exchange your cash for an equivalent value of a precious metal – gold and silver are typical. The price of the metal may change by the time you wish to exchange it back into currency, but it is considered a more stable investment. I don't see this as much better than stocks and shares in that you have no control over its value.

Property is something that you can buy, enhance, control and use. Above all, you can ask to raise a loan against its value and increase the return that you get from it. Again, we come back to the point about a relatively small island with high demand for land. I'll use an example of property to show you both leverage in a simple form and how income is generated.

If you imagine having £200,000 cash (or released as equity from your home), you have a few choices:

You might be able to buy one house outright in outer London for that amount and live in it. You would get no rental income as you are the tenant so your wages would pay for the mortgage.

What if you bought the house outright and placed a tenant in the property to pay the rent? Because you have no mortgage all the rental income would be profit. If your tenants stay all year at £850 per month, that would be £10,200 per year.

What if you took your £200,000 and used a mortgage to leverage it so that you used only £50,000 as a deposit for each of four houses worth £200,000 each. Now you have to pay a mortgage of £150,000 at 5%, for example. That would take £7,500 per year out of your profit of £10,200, leaving a profit of £2,700 on each house. That's a grand total of £10,800 for all four properties. It's a bit better, but really only £600 a year more. In real life, you would have other buying costs such as solicitor, surveyor and broker fees.

Could we do better? What if instead of buying near London we went further north where property prices are cheaper? What if average house prices were £50,000 to make the maths easier? (In fact, I have bought property at £51,000 for two-bedroomed houses and I regularly buy at £55,000–65,000.)

I will be even more accurate now and say that each property requires £25,000 cash to cover the deposit on the property and all the costs of buying from fees and surveys to repairs and finding a tenant. Using a mortgage to leverage your money you could buy up to 8 properties with the same like-for-like 25% mortgage deposit. The total rent from a three-bedroomed house is about £6,600 per annum and the cost of the mortgage about £1,875.[33]

This would mean that each little house would give you £6,600, minus £1,875 mortgage costs = £4,725 profit per house. Multiple that by 8 houses = £37,800 per year profit compared to £10,800.

You can see the power of leverage in this example. In real life, the profits are lower (approximately 20%) because you need to allow for void periods and repairs, but the rates of return in London compared to the north of England is 3–7% compared to 10–15%[34] return. That is the power of leverage.

So, the question is, once you have decided on the life you want and you understand the resources you have, how can you make the most of them by

---

33 Please note I have used these figures to make the maths easier to read – but they are close to actual properties that I have bought. This is just a simple example. I have used a 5% interest rate for this model.

34 £37,800 less 20% costs = £30,240 divided by £200,000 invested - 15.2% ROI.

using leverage and outsourcing? The previous example is raw and illustrative, but I hope it makes the point.

As material possessions become less important and a house does not necessarily have to be a home, this shift will be fascinating to watch as it is bound to involve the clash of intergenerational values. Not just arguments in families, but politicians will be out of kilter and businesses will struggle to keep up.

Do you understand how your potential property investment model or strategy could give you the flexibility you want now and financial security for the future? It will be possible to work in partnership as a family to create this if you start to think about property differently – NOW!

Imagine if you invested in property today, at relatively low prices. That property would provide income to support the family as a whole until certain demands arose like school fees, university fees, business start-up costs, elderly parents or early retirement.

The main portfolio would remain as the core asset and all spending would come from the revenue the rental income generated. In approximately 10 years, the value of the portfolio would double – so you might make a decision to adapt your strategy. You could sell three of the 8 properties in the portfolio and use the capital released (3 x £100,000 to pay all the outstanding mortgages of 8 x £37,500 = £300,000) to give you (from our early example) 5 properties with no mortgages.

You might be worried that your income will reduce if you sell some of your portfolio, however if you use the capital to clear the mortgages then you would own 5 mortgage free properties that means 100% of the rental income is yours (less maintenance costs of course). Your new income based on the old figures would be as follows:

£200,000 to £800,000 in 10 years

8 x rent = £37,800 p.a.
less 20% allowance
for maintenance
and voids over 10 years
= £302,400

8 properties worth £50,000 with
£4,725 rental profit each = £302,400

After sale of 3 properties
5 owned outright
portfolio value £500,000
ongoing cashflow
5 x £550 = £33,000

You sell 3 properties for £300,000 and
pay back the mortgages (8x£37,500)
of £300,000

8 properties worth £50,000 with £4,725 rental profit each = £37,800.

You sell three properties for £300,000 and pay back the mortgages (8 x £37,500) of £300,000.

You now have five properties mortgage free.

Over the last ten years you would have released £200,000 of your cash or equity and through your understanding of the leverage and inflation strategy created a portfolio of 5 properties mortgage free worth a total of half a million pounds.

You would have received almost £302,400 of rental profit (£4,725 x 8 houses x ten years).

You would have ongoing cashflow of approximately £33,000 if all factors stayed the same.

You might be wondering about the original £200,000 – if that was released from your home with a mortgage how has that been paid? You have had £302,400 cashflow – you could use that. You could use the cashflow to add to the portfolio and buy more property and then clear everything at the end – it all depends on what you need to earn from property, what resources you have to start with and of course your approach towards risk, leverage and property management.

This is just an example. It is designed to get you thinking about property in a different way – one that suits the demand of future generations. Yes, for the detailed people, I made property value double and did not double the rent. So what if once all the numbers became precise you only earned £250,000 in 10 years for just making a decision today, or only had £25,000 extra per year without working? That's why I spend my time and money investing in property and why I help my clients to invest in property. That is how you can have a lifestyle of choice and ongoing financial security.

If you want to know how this would work for you personally, get in touch and we can arrange a resource audit and personal investment strategy session.

Lesson 6: letting go of old habits

This will probably be easier for your children than for you or your parents. Have you realised yet that the cold hard truth is that as a society we are bankrupt? Can you admit that you need to provide for your own future? Your lifestyle (as stressful as it has been in the past) will mean that you will live longer. You have seen your parents and grandparents start to struggle as they have to cut back to conserve cash reserve for when they get older. What sort of life and retirement do you want? What life do you want for your children and your grandchildren?

So now do you accept that it is time to invest in cashflowing property assets?

While you enjoy your share of technical gadgets, you also recognise the difference between good debt (money borrowed to buy income-generating assets) and bad debt (money borrowed or personal capital spent on material luxuries that then incur high interest rates as you cannot afford to clear the loans or credit cards). You know your next car will be funded by profit made from your tenants.

This means your path to a wealthier life is exponentially faster than your parents or peers who are still trapped selling their time for money, which never seems to be enough. It's a good job you are growing your wealth because you can see friends around you are starting to run out of money and they will need you to help them – to show them the way, before it's too late.

The best thing you did was read *Property for the Next Generation* and Robert Kiyosaki's book *Rich Dad, Poor Dad: What the Rich Teach Their Kids About Money That the Poor and Middle Class Do Not!* By releasing money from your house you were able to work with me and my team to start investing in property much sooner than your peers. Your healthy portfolio has provided the cashflow and feeling of security to enable you to make better decisions. Now you can focus on helping others.

Lesson 7: who is in your team?

Group work at school or university was always a nightmare of mismatched personalities, with different work ethics bound together and reliant on one another to get a good grade.

With a more fluid and actually less visible workforce, many working online or in different countries, personalities are less important than the quality of the work produced and the adherence to deadlines and profit targets. These are the classic markers that online work environments like Elance use.

In the past businesses have struggled to grow as increased sales means a greater staff team is needed. Employment legislation, tax and other costs of an employee were a huge commitment and prohibitive – now businesses often employ someone for a project and that is it. When the project is over the team member leaves. This means a business can grow opportunistically and adapt more easily to a volatile economic environment.

If you are already busy in your own business or job, then the ability to take on flexible and part time staff means you can leverage other people's time and grow your wealth. I have a financial director, a book keeper, a personal assistant, a social media expert, a publisher, an editor and a marketing and PR expert all as part of my team. They work a set number of hours or as part of a contract. They are not 'mine' exclusively, but they work to agreed deadlines and generate or save my income.

So have you identified your team? Who do you need to help you find, fix and fill a portfolio of cash-generating properties? Where in the country should you start? What property types should you look for? Who do you need in your team? Do you have the knowledge and understanding to make those decisions or do you need help with that too?

Do you know what you need to know?

This is the biggest question of all – who are you learning from? What are you learning? Is it relevant to the life you want to have and the world you are entering? Or is it from dusty tomes taught by people in the shadows rather than on the cutting edge of business?

Financial education is what matters. Understanding how leverage works as I showed you in the examples earlier (pages 57 and 63) matters. Understanding what ROI means and how you can compare the ROI for any decision you make matters. Understanding what your time is worth and what money is worth as a relative source of exchange matters.

Remember that time is also something that can be leveraged along with cash and, of course, knowledge. In Chapter 5, I explore case studies to help you envisage the different paths you can take to creating a property portfolio.

I will make one caveat, I do not know you or your personal circumstances. This is not financial advice. I am sharing my experience, knowledge and understanding in order to help you challenge traditional thinking. To help you develop your own goals that will give you and your family the sort of financial security and lifestyle you want.

If you would like to create your own personal investment strategy, then follow the lessons in this book:

- Review your personal financial position – think about what you are spending your money on and ask yourself if you could use it to build your financial security more easily if you leveraged it.

- Consider your actual asset, cash reserves and even equity in your own home, what rate of interest are you earning from your current financial strategies. Could you be earning more?

- Think about your time. Do you have time (or knowledge) to identify cashflowing property, often outside of the capital and large cities?

- Who can help you clarify and then achieve your goals?

There are resources and a newsletter to help you on my training company website (www.TheSourcersApprentice.com) for free and there is more information at the back of the book about how I can help.

Summary questions

1. What do you want? What do you value? What do you enjoy? Make a list.

2. Are you ready to take responsibility for the future you want? Complete a budget and work out what it will cost and how much you will need to earn.

3. Think about how you spend your time and what it's worth. Could you spend it more wisely?

4. Ask yourself if you need to spend money on the luxuries now, or if you could wait for your tenants to buy them for you?

5. Do you understand how business is changing and can you adapt to make the most of this opportunity?

6. Do you have an outline of a property investment strategy?

7. Who do you need in your team? Who do you need to talk to or meet with?

Chapter 4

What do you want in your life and how much will it cost?

Whether or not we consciously recognise it, we all want our lives to be like something. Our decisions have been influenced by the values and culture of our parents, peers and teachers. In a sense, we are bound by the reality of those around us, but is their reality relevant any more?

If you could start without any limitations or generational beliefs, what sort of life would you want? A good place to start is to think about what is important to you. What do you value? Having said this, a lot of your beliefs will still have been influenced by your parents.

So start a list. Think about what really matters to you in your life and, in turn, about the way that you earn a living. Is variety important? What about stability and structure? Is status important or knowing that you have done something that made a difference? We are all different and there is no need for judgement to be laid on these choices. It is just a 'conversation' about how you think you want to live the next 30–40 years of your adult life. For some, having a job and being part of a team or an organisation is comforting, satisfying and fulfilling; the idea of working alone and motivating yourself every day seems unnecessarily unpleasant.

Other people think that work means constraint, routine and rules – that's another opinion. It also might mean responsibility, commitment, achievement and self-motivation. Know what you want to get out of life and what you value. These intrinsic values shape the choices you make.

Another area to consider is your lifestyle needs. Again, there are no judgements. Do you want to travel, grow your family, work in a city or 'make things'? Does technology excite you? Would you like to work and live with lots of people, or do you prefer numbers or a quieter life? What about sports, hobbies, social life, music, gadgets, cars and possessions, or are you more of a wandering spirit who prefers not to be burdened by possessions? You may love your current job and want to keep it no matter how much you earn, or you may have always wanted to open an art gallery, cake shop or even offer cruises on your own boat.

The answers to the above questions serve only to outline the potential cost of maintaining your desired lifestyle. Costs and plans that you will adapt over time as relationships change along with the world around you. To start with, if your lifestyle is more complex with more material or expensive desires, then your way of making money will need to work towards that. However, if your lifestyle is more simple – uncluttered with a few bits of technology to support you – then you will have a different budget.

Ultimately, the message of this book is that you need to take responsibility for the life and lifestyle you want to have. You need to prepare your children for a future that is less economically certain than the past and, more importantly, a future that is not financially backed by a government with limitless pockets. You need to help your children prepare for a more mobile, technological and fast-paced world.

So now the task is to identify your resources and notice how you are currently allocating them. Are your resources working for you or for someone else? Really, this is just a question of mindset. Let's think about the resources in broad terms: money; time; health; and emotional energy.

Money – you can spend, save or invest

The question here is about the value versus the worth of the money. Money has a value on its 'face' – it is called one pound or five pounds. Imagine a hot day, perhaps you are in a park and a passing salesman offers you a bottle of water for a pound. Is it worth it? Yes. What if he charged £4? Would it still be worth it? It depends how hot and thirsty you are. On a hot day that water might be worth four times the cost on a colder day. The face value stays the same but it's worth to you changes.

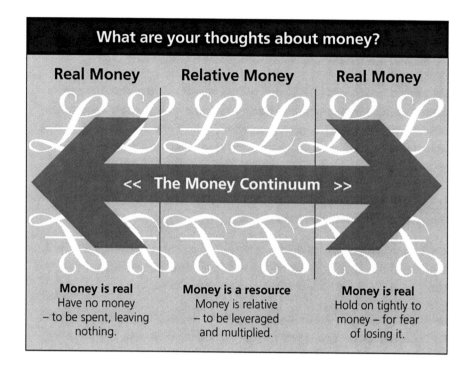

What are your thoughts about money?

Real Money   **Relative Money**   **Real Money**

<< **The Money Continuum** >>

Money is real
Have no money
– to be spent, leaving
nothing.

Money is a resource
Money is relative
– to be leveraged
and multiplied.

Money is real
Hold on tightly to
money – for fear
of losing it.

When people see money as real they want to hold on to it. For some, the more they grab the less they have and, for others, the more they save the less its worth because of the decisions they make. This is where having the right sort of financial education is crucial. Think about the very rich. What do they own a lot of? The answer is property and land. This is because we are an island with a finite supply, therefore it will always be of value and/or worth to someone.

What has happened to pensioners over recent years since the start of the latest recession during 2007–2008? Their pensions and savings based on stocks, shares and the stock market first shot up and then they were slashed as share prices fell! What if they had just held on to the cash in a pot by their bed? Then it would have lost between 4–5% of its value in real terms each year because prices rose due to inflation but their money stayed the same.

What if they had put the money in the bank? Well, they might have been getting 1–2% interest, maybe 3% if they were lucky (subject to certain conditions) but they were still losing out overall against inflation.

They could have invested in property. If they had bought before the crash, then their property's worth compared to someone else's might have fallen, but a property's value lies in the rental income it generates. As long as they have a tenant, then their property is still worth the same to them!

If you consider money as an exchange mechanism – something to be exchanged – then you can start to see that you can put it to work for you and that is what I will explain in Chapter 5.

The biggest problem with money is that once you have spent the money it is gone – it leaves your hands and passes to another person. Most often, it is exchanged for something that you valued at the time.

Look at the example about buying a coffee from a coffee shop on page 52. The example shows that if you spend your money on a latte every day for 21 days you would have spent £57.75, but you would have lost the opportunity to make millions. Surely you'll never buy another coffee again.

In the title of this chapter I ask the question: how much will it cost? (i.e. this lifestyle of yours). This is relatively easy to budget. Take all the expenses in your life and the projected expenses of any business or immediate additional outlay and complete an income and expenses budget. Tracking your money on a monthly basis is a brilliant way to maintain focus. If you don't have a budget, then please download a copy from the resource page at: www. TheSourcersApprentice.com.

The real answer to the question 'how much will it cost?' depends on whether you are spending money you have to earn or whether you are spending money that has been made to work for you and is time-free cash.

So, as a final set of questions:

- Can you now see that you can invest your financial resources in such a way that money could be seen as your 'employee', i.e. its sole job is to earn you money? You would have control over the decisions and results surrounding its use and you would have the ability to influence how much it earned.

- Do you now see that money is not real but has, in effect, a relative value based on how it is used? There is a decision to make about whether money continues to be spent in the short term, on material objects for example, or invested (put to work) to earn cashflow that could then be used to buy things while maintaining the value of the capital sum.

Time – you can spend it, save it or invest it

So you have a clear idea of the type of lifestyle you want and you have costed this on a spreadsheet. You are starting to get curious about money – what is it worth compared to its face value and how can you make it work for you? You start to question whether money is real or relative, especially as you understand that it is most likely to be based on debt anyway! Now you need to think about how you want to spend your time as another one of your valuable assets.

Once you are in control of your money then the next resource you can think about is your time. Once the burden of exchanging your time for money is removed and it is replaced with the constant flow of cash from assets bought with your goals in mind, then your whole way of thinking changes. You can actually start to revisit those long forgotten goals of travel, business, hobbies or childish dreams.

Time is like money in that we give it a unitary value of hours and minutes. However, does the hour spent on the train with lots of hot commuters have the same value as the hour a soldier returning from duty abroad spends with their son or daughter for the first time in six months or a year?

Time is worse than money in that we, as individuals, only have a finite amount. You can always borrow money from someone else, but when you borrow an hour you don't really get it – you just give what you were going to do to someone else. This is why you need to think carefully about the value of your time and how you spend it. Do you spend your time doing a job you love, either working for yourself or for someone else, or doing a job you hate?

The great thing about the internet is that it speeds things up – you can now get information at your fingertips. You can work from home and save commuting. You can do online banking and online shopping and save queuing and travel time. But what are you doing with the time you save? Add these ideas to your list of things that are important to you and that you enjoy.

Health and emotional energy – the foundation to your success

Without good health or emotional resilience you will struggle. These are more important than money and time combined. A doctor can make you better, but only you can make yourself sick. The stress you bring into your life and the food that you eat all contribute to the levels of hormones and chemicals in your body. How are you spending your life? Because that's what we are actually talking about!

A quick word on emotional resilience here because you will need this in bucket loads if you decide that property investment or working for yourself is your path. Resilience is vital if you are to overcome challenges, to work every day when you need to, to make those tough calls and hard decisions and, for some people, to actually make a sales call or do the accounts! Even more important is the resilience to ignore the comments of doomsayers who are not educated like you, but rely on the old teachings of school and the *Daily Mirror*.

So now you can see your life in terms of resources that you can spend or invest. The next question is can you let go of old habits…?

Chapter 5

Teach your 22-year-old to buy their own house

In Chapter 2, I explained how everything we thought to be true and real is actually shifting under our feet. The government cannot fulfil the promises made by generations of years gone by. 2012 saw the 60th anniversary and Jubilee year of the Queen's reign.

During that time, 12 prime ministers have failed to recognise that the books just don't balance; that as a country (and now it seems as a world) we are spending so much more than we can ever possibly hope to repay. We are in fact spiralling into debt. If our country was a family and the government were the parents, then we would hope one of the adults would notice what was wrong and do something about it!

In 1954, we shared different values and beliefs – I think born of the fact that life was tough. The population was not reliant on handouts from the government in return for nothing. The demands on our health service were not as strained as they are now with the burgeoning obesity crisis, cancer and other extreme diseases. ME or 'yuppie flu' had not been recognised, nor had attention deficit disorders. Back then, it was not possible to cure many illnesses with a simple pill or 'key-hole' surgical procedure and, in doing so, extend the lives of thousands of people.

Today, there is pressure to put every child through free education, regardless of their capability or future aspirations. There is the added pressure of an increasingly ageing population reliant on the government to support them for 10, 20 or even 30 years after retirement. The system cannot continue.

In Chapter 3, I systematically described the seven lessons they will not be teaching your child in school. I explained how money is really debt and, therefore, if you don't keep it moving it actually loses value as the rate of inflation erodes your asset and equity.

In Chapter 4, I explained how we should think about money differently – see it as a tool that we can master and make work for us.

Money can either cost you a fortune (literally if you don't manage the accumulating debt) or enable you to live a comfortable life free from worry or stress.

Learning to spend from earned income rather than capital will mean that you have your own personal cash generating machine for generations to come. Use credit cards and fail to manage the interest costs and you will end up working for the banks in order to clear your debt.

In this chapter, I will explain different strategies that you can use to create your family portfolio, from buying a single investment property to teaching your child to buy a property portfolio that will enable them to have lifelong financial freedom.

I will show you a model if your children are under 16 or 17 years olds, where you can take advantage of the slump in the property market to get in at the 'bottom' and watch as the increasing value of your portfolio effectively erodes your debt while generating cash to pay school fees, university fees or give you flexibility and security.

Case study 1: save up and buy it yourself

As with anything I do (either with clients or for myself) I need to know 'why?' I don't see this as an emotional process – so many people buy 'homes' based on love or some other emotion. This is a brilliant investment. Having said this, I recognise that buying a property for the first time may be exciting, scary, confusing even. My aim is to approach this as a business investment that you may or may not live in – an investment that you will not sell, an investment that will grow in value and generate enough income to pay for itself.

This is the story of how my daughter, Kimberley, set her mind to buy her first property at the age of 22 years old. Before I start in detail, I think it is important to say that this model worked because I encouraged her to go through the thinking process outlined in Chapter 4 on page 71. She decided what she wanted in her life and what resources she had access to – including checking with me about possible financial handouts (and it was fair that she asked – it is what young people have been taught). She then identified her resource gap and set about dealing with it. It was successful because it was driven by her and not by me.

So why does your child want to buy a property? It's crucial that they can answer this question. It might be a simple answer, such as 'I want to leave home'. In an ideal world, your children might like to live near work or university, but it is important to check affordability. I will explain this later.

'Why?' speaks to the motivation for the purchase and, as I mentioned in Chapter 2, Myth 6 on page 31, some young people have spent the last three years or more reading the press that explains how they can't afford to invest. All the while, television programmes such as *Homes Under the Hammer* and presenters such as Sarah Beeny demonstrate how you can buy property cheaply and sell it on for a massive profit. That is why I asked about the underlying motivation.

If the desire is to follow the television programmes and invest for a capital return (get a lump sum on the sale of the property), then explaining about income-generating assets, spending from revenue rather than capital and all the figures from Chapter 1 relating to future rising house prices should show them that this is never an easy, or necessarily simple, strategy to follow.

Let's move past the motivation for a minute and start to look at what they want to buy. Now, in some parts of the country house prices might be dictating your choices, or rather limiting them. It's important to look at a few house types through the eyes of a professional investor and consider their functionality, suitability and value for money.

Creating and managing a credit score

As discussed in Chapter 3, Lesson 1 on page 43, lenders use credit scores as a way of calculating how likely a person is to pay or default on a loan. My daughter and I addressed this immediately. Kimberley was open to ideas and instruction because a good credit score is so important and yet so easy to ruin.

All of Kimberley's credit cards were already on direct debits, as we had previously discussed finance as and when the topic came up. So now we obtained copies of her credit scores and credit reports from the main agencies. Her scores were high and clean, so no repair work was needed. If you find that credit scores for people in your family home are damaged and poor, it can reflect on the entire family.

Affordability

Next, we spoke about location and property type in a general way to get a sense of the goal and whether or not it was realistic. I understood that maximum mortgage loans are calculated on a multiple of the family income – so three, four or five times a salary can be loaned. These figures can be based on a joint wage as well as a single income.

I gave Kimberley a rough maximum purchase price based on her salary. So, for example, if someone earned £25,000 per annum and the multiplier was four times their salary, then they could borrow a maximum of £100,000. Now that is the maximum loan and could represent 95% or even 90% of the purchase price – let's take 90%.

So £100,000 (potential maximum loan) divided by 90 (the loan to value ratio of the mortgage) x 100 (to help calculate the actual property asking price) = approximately £111,111.

This means a young person could view properties that were for sale between £111,000–125,000 with a view to offering a purchase price of £111,111, knowing that a lender would lend 90% of the purchase price (i.e. £99,999) and that their salary would meet the affordability conditions of the loan.

Property types

It is important to understand property as an investment (even though if bought as a home it will be a liability). There are cost implications to property types.

Flats

The challenge with flats is both structural and financial. Looking at the structural issues, every property in the block is likely to be broadly the same. This makes differentiation more difficult when it comes to either selling or renting it out for an income that you want.

You cannot easily change the windows (there may be rules imposed by the managing agent or the freeholder) or change the front door and you certainly cannot put on an extension. This means opportunities to add value through structural change is almost zero.

If your property is part of a block, there will also be overheads for managing the property such as keeping communal areas clean, light and maintained. There are costs such as management and accounting to run the managing agency. This is where the financial challenge occurs as there are limitations to your power to influence the repairs or repair costs as everyone involved with the block will have to agree.

Houses

Now consider a house. Even on a street of similar properties, you as the freeholder can change the doors and windows or add an extension to the roof or rear (subject to local council approval). You are in charge of the maintenance and upkeep without the need for management costs.

New-build houses

A new-build house compared to an older property certainly can prove a buying challenge for young people, especially if, as parents, you have been inclined to repeatedly buy older properties and do them up to sell and start the process again. New-build properties will most likely offset a greater level of comfort and 'ready-to-move-in' marketing against actual floor space. Older properties, even 1960s ex-council properties, will appear significantly larger than their equivalent new-build house. Floor space as well as height of the ceilings can give a much larger feel to a room.

The second challenge comes from the same problem we see in flats – differentiation. If the new-build property is on a new estate, then making it stand out from a neighbour's property may be difficult. The other devil in the detail of new-build properties is the 'ready-made' nature of them. The purchase price includes the carpeting and the cost of the fridge. So when you borrow your loan to buy the bricks and mortar you are also paying 3–5% for 20+ years on the cost of a fridge.

After 25 years, a fridge that would have cost £250 could have almost doubled in cost as mortgage interest rates last 25 years instead of just the two or three years offered by Curry's or Argos!

Of course, buying an older house can be more challenging, especially if renovation works and updating are required. However, it may simply be a case of redecoration, which all helps in the process of adding value.

Making the right move

By using online search sites such as rightmove.co.uk you can search for property that your child could theoretically afford to buy. By entering a postcode or town, choosing the property type (one, two or three bedroomed) and setting a maximum value of £125,000, the search engine returned a list of properties that matched our criteria. If this does not work in the precise location you want to live, extend the search radius from a quarter of a mile to one mile, and so on. Understandably, in London this will cover a massive area of properties.

It can take some time to refine the searching process, but in the end possible postcodes and affordable areas start to emerge. The next stage is to think about the consequences of that area compared to travel to work and travel to friends, family and social life. Ultimately, everyone wants a home that is convenient for all aspects of their lives. Parents will consider the impact of local schools, for instance.

Alongside the task of checking credit scores and learning about online searching, we discussed savings and other financial assets. Kimberley completed the income and expenses budget that is available through www. TheSourcersApprentice.com. This gave us a clear picture of her cashflow. We calculated what was true while she lived at home and worked out what would change when she left home. For example:

- rent or housekeeping would become mortgage payments
- she would have utility bills, council tax and household insurance to pay
- food costs would be joined by cleaning products and toiletries
- she would need the funds to furnish the property, not just large items such as a cooker or fridge but everything from corkscrews and potato peelers to plates and sheets.

I honestly think working through catalogues and online stores to plan and cost everything needed for Kimberley's home was a reward after completing the income and expenses sheet. She became an expert at finding deals and gradually buying items as they came on sale over the two years it took her to move from starting to look to finding and buying her first home.

By the time Kimberley had her purchase offer accepted, she already had a chest full of all the minor household items and only needed to order white goods, a sofa and bed.

So, the process included:

1. Manage and monitor your credit score.
2. Calculate your income and expenses and make adjustments in order to save the 5–10% deposit required. If you are determined and already live at home, then two years of hard saving, thinking about expenses and shifting all birthday and Christmas presents towards your goal of owning your own home is very achievable.
3. Calculate what you can afford to borrow – not just with the affordability calculator but by actual thinking about the impact on your personal income and expenses in real life.

4. Calculate what you can afford to buy based on what you can afford to borrow.
5. Define your target area. Where can you reasonably afford to live and does that make sense?
6. Budget and plan for household goods while saving for your deposit.

When you do get to the stage of viewing properties and defining your area, carry out the following simple checks:

1. What is the area like at 8 am on a weekday morning, 10 pm on a Saturday evening and 11 am on a Sunday morning? By visiting the area at different times you can see the impact of school and work traffic on the surrounding roads during and out of rush hour. Are local pubs noisy and what about church bells?
2. Practise your new route to work. Do so on a weekday during rush hour, so leave home early, drive to your new target home area and then on to work – this will be a really valuable lesson.
3. Finally, think about your habits. Do you belong to a gym? If so, where is it in relation to your new home? Are you on a course? If so, how will the travelling impact on your studies? Where is your nearest shop? Are there local superstores or smaller convenience stores that you could use?

The buying process

The second phase is learning about property and the buying process – what questions to ask. The fact that I am a professional property investor and buy property for a living was an advantage. We waited until Kimberley had saved the 10% deposit, plus enough money to buy a bed, fridge, cooker, etc. and pay for a survey and broker and solicitor fees. This came to a total of £24,000.

To achieve a savings rate of £1,000 per month, Kimberley's social life adapted. Fun included going for walks and buying memberships to both a cinema and a gym. Friends could all then meet for free and train, swim, go for a sauna and visit the cinema for a low monthly fee. She also spent a lot of time meeting at the houses or flats of friends who had already bought property. She had a goal and was focused on achieving it.

We knew that Kimberley's target mortgage was a maximum of £180,000 – it worked both in terms of affordability according to the lender and her own personal budget. So we knew that based on a 90% mortgage she could buy a property for £200,000 and we could even shop a bit higher and negotiate.

Therefore, if you start out knowing that you want to negotiate you need to know what situation the vendor is in:

- How long has the house been on the market? (The longer the better as this means the vendor might be more keen to move.)
- Where are they moving to? (Do they already have somewhere in mind and so are keen to move, or are they not in a rush?)
- Why are they moving? (Could be to meet schooling needs of children, due to divorce, family sickness or work related.)

Every question, asked conversationally as we walked around the house, was designed to calculate how quickly the vendor wanted to move and therefore how likely they were to accept an offer on their asking price.

Viewing like a surveyor

Looking at a property in a dispassionate and non-emotional way, like a mortgage surveyor, is a vital skill. What condition is the roof in, the chimney, gutters or soffits? What is the condition of the windows and general exterior? All these questions indicate the cost of immediate or future repairs.

Inside is easier as it will fall under the heading of 'general decoration' (after all, it is likely that most people will want to repaint before they move in) and then 'key expense items' like the electrics, heating system and state of the bathroom and kitchen – what condition are they in? Most families know someone who understands a bit about building. Therefore, once a shortlist of potential properties is compiled, invite someone to come with you. If not me or a relative, then ask a local builder.

Ask the estate agent any questions that you don't or can't ask the vendor. In most cases, the homeowner will have gone out to allow the estate agent to carry out the viewing anyway.

So, after saving the amount needed, the lesson moves on to property management and conditioning – get help if you need it. Above all, consider the type of survey you get when you buy the property. The cheapest surveys are just valuations for the use of the lender. If you do not have access to family or friends with property expertise, then invest in a more expensive but reassuring full-structural survey.

The mechanics of buying

As a parent and homeowner you probably know the actual mechanics of buying. I explicitly explained the process to my daughter. I explained about offering on a property and the acceptance of an offer, the questions and information the solicitor would need, the information and process of applying for a mortgage and, finally, the process of exchange and completion.

You, as a parent, will know a lot of this but there are three points I would like to highlight:

1. If you don't talk your children through the whole process, they will be unable to prepare themselves or ask the right questions.
2. Think like a property investor. This property will now stay in the family for a considerable amount of time. The best time to make money on a property is when you buy it for the lowest price possible. Be prepared to make your offer and, if not accepted, walk away. If you are not buying with an emotional 'head', then this process will be easier and you will get a better deal.
3. Above all, be polite and respectful. Unless you are buying a repossession, you will be walking around someone's home. Whether or not it is the right price or suits your taste, imagine the owner is in the room with you.

So, if it is that relatively easy to buy a property, what next? Explain to your children that they could continue to maximise their income and expenses and work out how much they can save towards their next property. You will not be able to rely on property price increases and remortgages (and I would counsel against overuse of that strategy), but once you have satisfied your desire to buy a 'home' the next property can be bought with tenants in mind.

So, in summary, the 'save up and buy' model is as follows:

A Understand personal spending and cashflow budgets.
B Know how much you can borrow.
C Work out where you can afford to live.
D Research.
E Save.
F Look.
G Buy.
H Do it again.

Living the dream

I have to say that buying her first house was an act of extreme determination on Kimberley's part. She knew what she wanted, she worked out what she had to do and she did it. Yes, there were times when I saw her go out two nights in a row (shock) or buy a new pair of shoes (bigger shock), but she found a way to work hard, play sensibly and get what she wanted quickly.

This is why I started with the question 'why?' Once your child knows why they want their own home or investment property they will be determined to achieve it.

Case study 2: starting young

This is less a case study and more a story of a family that has enabled their children to explore an adult world.

I knew one of my clients long before I helped her to invest. Every event we met at her daughter, Ruby, was there by her side. Not because the mum was a single parent with no one to look after her daughter, but because her daughter was interested in what her mum got up to.

I have known Ruby for over four years now. In the early days, she brought her colouring books, then, later, a Gameboy to keep herself entertained during the two or three-hour long property meeting. Between the ages of 9 and 12, she even attended three-day events and heard Robert Kiyosaki,

Daniel Priestley and Tony Robbins amongst others speak about money, business economics and success. This year she listened to Donald Trump, Adam Ginsberg and others.

Now, Ruby is comfortable in the company of adults and is like a smaller member of the group, able to hold a confident conversation in her own right. Most importantly she is gaining an education in finance, business and world economics like no other child in her school. I can't help but see that as an advantage, not an advantage over others but an advantage for her in her life and her future.

Of course on top of all this her mum is a successful entrepreneur, who started her own business after we worked together to create her cashflowing property.

Case study 3: the willing teenager

A mentee and business partner of mine has enabled and encouraged his 15-year-old daughter, Laura, to join him at our property events. Laura comes with her father, enjoys the dinner and joins property investors at a table to listen to a variety of speakers. She is starting to read property books and ask questions.

I know it is only a matter of months before she sits at a table with other investors (separate from her father) and holds her own conversations and asks her own questions. She is already starting to think through what she wants in life and how she might achieve it. I can see that she is already starting to question whether A-levels and university is the quickest path.

At a recent entrepreneurial event Laura listened to business entrepreneurs like Daniel Priestley of Entrevo, Mike Harris founder of Egg, First Direct and Garlik, Penny Power founder of Ecademy.com and now the Digital Youth Academy and Shaa Wasmund founder of Smarta.com. She heard about their journeys into entrepreneurial thinking and she heard what they think is critical in business today. Laura is now thinking about her book and her business.

Did I mention that my daughter was kicked out of school for not handing in A-level coursework on time? Now, just seven years later she runs a team of five staff and has her own home with no other significant loans to clear!

Case study 4: follow a career path

The children of two friends have both taken a practical approach to learning about property investment by getting jobs in the business: one as a letting agent; the other as an estate agent.

There are many reasons why this is a brilliant apprenticeship for any young person thinking that they want to make a career out of property investment. First, because of the practical sales experience, and, second, because of the research and contacts that they can accumulate.

Depending on where a person actually works, they can get experience of the property types, the client types and the types of questions and challenges associated with setting up a business around sourcing (finding) property deals for other investors. This is the core message behind my second book, *Make More Money from Property: From investor thinking to a business mindset*.

Case study 5: building a portfolio for the next generation

One of my clients has a young family and his wife stays at home to look after them. After we spoke about his situation and his plans, he made the decision to realise some of the equity in his property. I helped him use that money to invest in a property portfolio.

The properties provide some additional income now but more importantly they are a legacy for his children. Maybe he was thinking ahead to when the children grow up and want to attend university. With three to send that could become very expensive very quickly.

The model is very similar to the one I used when I released equity from my parents' home (page 55) in that the rent pays the mortgages and the profit pays for the equity release. The remaining profit adds to the family income.

This model can be adapted to any amount of equity released for investment purposes as long as the rental income can afford to pay for the mortgage on the buy-to-let (investment) property and the equity release mortgage while still leaving a profit.

If having additional income right now is not important to you but leaving a legacy for your children or developing your own pension pot is a priority then the model still works as accrued cashflow can be reinvested into more properties on an annual basis.

Case study 6 – investing for the future

I am working with a client who has a million pounds to invest (most clients start with £100,000). We are planning a wider portfolio strategy that would see the total portfolio being a combination of smaller buy-to-let properties in, say, the north west where we can get 12% return on investment easily, and then combining that with some larger properties that become houses of multiple occupancy (HMOs) let to five to eight individual sharers, maybe professionals, students or even migrant workers.

The critical decision in the planning process I have been working on with the client is to minimise risk and exposure.

Minimising risk requires a balance of grouping properties together to benefit from economies of scale with build teams and letting agents and having a balance of strategies so some properties let as single dwellings and some as HMOs.

Minimising exposure means limiting the number of times that you remortgage a property. I personally believe that property can provide an indefinite return of cashflow for generations to come by letting inflation effectively reduce the debt on the property as prices rise (see Chapter 3, Lesson 3 on page 58). This means that the overall loan to value of the portfolio should aim to be below 75% and as prices start to rise this will reduce to 50% and less. If you keep remortgaging property every time it increases in value, you not only reduce the cashflow but you increase the risk of exposure.

With this client we will probably end up with a portfolio like this:

- 8 buy-to-let houses costing (worst case scenario) £240,000 to buy.
- 12 HMOs costing (worst case scenario) £720,000 to buy. That's a total of £960,000, leaving £40,000 for contingencies or to follow another strategy.

Cashflow would be as follows:

- 8 buy-to-lets giving £250 per month = £24,000 per annum.
- 12 HMOs giving £700 per month (£850 is possible but being conservative) = £100,800 per annum.

That's a monthly income of £10,400.

The future – is up to you

These are just a few of the examples. The key point here is that you don't know what you could do until you ask the right questions. Whatever amount you start with, whether it's a single buy-to-let that costs £30,000 to get going and helps out your family budget by another £3,000 a year or releasing a million pounds and creating a family portfolio. You will be creating a plan based on your personal circumstances for the life you want and that is what is so important. Please consider why you are investing before you start and make sure that you discuss this with your family and your new property team.

Whether your children read property investment books like mine, wealth and mindset books like Robert Kiyosaki or the books detailing why the adults have got the economy in a mess like Simon Dixon and others in the Bibliography (see page 103), help them when they show an interest. Have conversations about money: explain what interest is and what it costs; what an asset is and what a liability is; how once you have spent money from your capital it is gone, but invest your capital and spend the profit and the capital will keep laying the golden eggs. Help them to understand because we need them to get the country and the world out of this debt mess.

On the next page I go right back to the beginning. For those of you who are interested, I explain how I learnt about money, wealth and property and all those fascinating things that school didn't teach me.

Maybe my story will inspire you to want to know more, or to share and talk to your children. Perhaps it might inspire you to get in touch to see how we can help you create a property portfolio for the next generation and prepare your family for a wealthy future.

Appendix

My story and how I learnt what school will never teach you

I will briefly explain my story, so you can understand the real value in this book and why I am so passionate about sharing this knowledge. My story is relevant in that it will help you to understand why I was driven to learn and what experience I have, and why I was driven to write this book. It will add the context – the richness and the drama. If you read carefully between the lines, you will also see how our world was changing irrevocably as I wrote: the globalness, the interconnectedness, business and money knowing no borders or boundaries and how that is continuing to impact implicitly and unconsciously on our everyday lives.

The simpler life of a child

Without dwelling on the past for too long, I was a happy and perhaps privileged child by some people's standards. I used the word 'privileged' because I don't remember wanting for anything; I don't remember seeing my parents struggle. As an adult, I can now reflect on how hard they worked: my father as a tailor, ultimately getting his own shop; and my mother first as a shop owner and then working in the bar and restaurant trade to fit her hours around school times. We had a foreign holiday every year as we travelled across Europe by car (a little Fiat 500) to Italy to see my father's sister and family.

I lived in a world (not too long ago) where I was happy to get an orange and my Girl Guide's Book wrapped up from Father Christmas. The X-Box, iPad, branded, labelled, technological world had not impacted on my need for material things. Life was easier and simpler and, dare I say it, cheaper – and I am really not that old!

I also don't remember ever hearing phrases like 'money doesn't grow on trees' or 'money is the root of all evil'. I had no feelings attached to money – it really was not on my radar.

While I loved playing with the tills in my parents' shops, and I worked with them from around the age of 12 years, I was not overtly entrepreneurial – I didn't create business ideas and sell things to friends. I got my first 'official' Saturday job at 16 and enjoyed it. I saved up and bought an expensive camera and then, as soon as I could, I bought my first car – they were functional rather than luxuries. I wanted to go to Portsmouth to study underwater photography (like Jacques Cousteau). Money was a tool. Money was accessible.

The downside of my 'privileged' life was that my family never discussed money or managing money in front of me. I had no concept of budgeting or saving. As an adult, again, I realise that they must have managed their money carefully because we were not rich in the financial sense but we lived a rich life. I can actually remember my mother buying that extra tin of Spam®, ham or corned beef (yuck) each week in the shopping so she could take it with us on our holiday. It meant that we could feed ourselves (self-catering) rather than go out to eat all the time. And I have a vague recollection of my father having a budget for each day of the holiday.

Money? Not a clue

So when I got married and my husband 'managed the money' (because that's what men seemed to do), I was surprised, unaware and deeply embarrassed when we nearly got repossessed because he had not been paying the mortgage. How could I have let this happen? Worse? I started to see a pattern...

Before we married, he didn't pay the rent on the flat we briefly shared and we were forced to move. Our first home was sold just before the bailiffs came and then our second home was sold the day before we were repossessed, while I was in hospital having our daughter as the stress in the final weeks brought on an early labour. I am not abdicating responsibility;

at this time I had no awareness of the importance of taking responsibility – financial or otherwise.

What was I thinking? I honestly don't know! Money was just not on my radar. As you can imagine, that all changed – it had to change!

Hard lessons about money

The first set of lessons came as the marriage broke up in violence and I fled to my parents with two baby daughters. I slept in their back room for a month or so while I tried to sort out my life emotionally, financially and literally. I was lucky, there was still the council system of housing people and I was shipped off to Brent to live in social housing.

I now know that the owner of the house that became our home for nearly three years had given their property over to the housing association on a lease. We were finally moved back to Uxbridge as we were ultimately their responsibility and we are still living in that house today.

Between 1991 and 1999 life settled down to a routine of financial budgeting and money management on a scale I had never yet experienced. I would imagine that some families are starting to put this in place now as the impact of the recession starts to hit households.

I literally counted every penny. I worked five jobs while studying my first degree and then 'just' two jobs during my Master's. During term-time, I taught in front of students for 30 hours a week, which meant another 60 hours of preparation and marking had to be squeezed in. My daughters became very disciplined and went to bed early (by today's standards) so that I could study for my Master's degree or mark students' work.

I saved for holidays and managed a trip to the Maldives, where I finally qualified as a scuba diver – my absolute passion. And then saved again and took the girls, then aged seven and nine to South Africa on the road trip of a lifetime. For six weeks we travelled from Capetown to Durban and places in between. The experience of visiting the KwaZulu Natal region in the east of South Africa had a profound effect on all three of us as we learnt what it really meant to be poor. Family units devoid of males (they leave to find work in the city) and, governed by the great grandmother, survive in circular thatched huts, gathering fire wood, rubbish to recycle and living in hand-me-down clothes. However you may feel right now, know that you are still one of the richest people in the world simply because you can afford to buy this book.

Making money work for me – the start

I mentioned that I learnt how to work credit cards to my benefit. I enhanced this skill so that by the time 0% credit cards became available we were able to buy our home from the council and 'offset' my mortgage interest by borrowing money on credit cards and holding it in a linked savings account.

I actually borrowed money for nothing and used it to offset the cost of my mortgage at 5–6% saving over £7,000 per year. I have an ebook that explains my understanding of how credit cards can work to your advantage, you can download it at: www.TheSourcersApprentice.com. If you still have questions, get in touch, drop me an email or a Facebook message.

However, I was still an employee with no idea about how money really worked. I was just stumbling on to strategies and using common sense to make them work. I recognised how I could borrow money for free, while other people were borrowing the cheap money and using it to buy material possessions, increasing their actual debt.

I honestly think that my failed marriage and time as a single mother gave me the skills to manage money that has proved invaluable throughout the rest of my life and the lives of my children. It is not something that I would recommend – as you read this book you gained an understanding of what I learnt without the pain and trauma of divorce!

On 9 of September 1999, life took another turn. I broke my arm while out on a bike ride and was rescued by Bob from the side of the road. We have been together ever since – my own knight in lycra (not really because we were hard core off-road cyclists covered in mud – but he is still my hero). Now I had a partner in my life again, but still no real idea about money, the future or anything.

Over the next seven years I would move from being a part-time/contract lecturer working six or seven contracts at a time to a job funded by government on an annual basis. This would be a massive change in terms of job security for me, certainly compared to the university. But, still, as a family we never completely knew what was happening financially for more than six months at a time. So budgeting and being 'careful' with money was still an underlying theme.

Redundancy and a change of direction

Then, in late 2005, I found out that funding for our quango was to stop and in the summer of 2006 I was made redundant. I had loved all my jobs and particularly loved this period. I had been working with education providers at a strategic level to shape education to meet the needs of local people. I worked with professional refugees as a director of a charity helping them to requalify and I sat on the board of directors of another government-funded regeneration project looking at the whole scale regeneration of South Kilburn in West London – this involved working on issues like housing, education, crime and 'young people'.

In late 2006, I had a go at being a consultant, but found I was working for free for all the people who used to work with me when I was funded by the government – that was technically a period of unrecognised unemployment and totally unsustainable! We must have tightened our family budget, changed our habits to account for having less income. I have no real memory of this – money was not really on my radar.

I am sharing this detail so that you can see I am just an ordinary person living an ordinary life. My experiences have taught me lessons that would become so valuable that they enabled me to become successful as a property investor. More importantly, I have created a property portfolio that will provide security for my family in a time when uncertainty, redundancy and financial insecurity dominates the news.

Retraining my mind

In 2007, I discovered personal development and I learnt how the mind worked. How we have a subconscious mind that is designed to protect us, and even a higher or spiritual mind that can inspire us. I welcomed the opportunity to explicitly learn again and soon qualified as a Master NLP practitioner (Neurolinguistic Programming) and hypnotherapist.

More important than the paper-based qualifications, I became a master of my own mind. I started to recognise how the guilt I felt for the failure of my marriage and its subsequent impact on my daughters was shaping everything I did. I was so focused on helping others, students at university, business and education providers through the Learning Partnership and then the residents of South Kilburn that I was not paying any attention to the long-term needs of my family (and perhaps not paying attention to their immediate needs either).

Some people I speak to feel uncomfortable with the idea of increasing their personal wealth. I am sorry to say, in my opinion, that's rubbish. We all need to increase our personal wealth – to become self-sustainable and to stop relying on the government to help because it just can't afford it any more!

In 2007, I had no savings and actually had nearly £80,000 on credit cards. Now I started to recognise that I had no job either. So I used my credit cards again to pay for my personal development and support me through the training. While that made my material debt worse, it paid off all my emotional debt and cleared the path for a truly wealthy life.

Somewhere along the way I read an incredible book by James Redfield called *The Celestine Prophecy*. It told the story of a young man on a journey and how he learnt that there were messages and signs all around him – opportunities if you like – and his lesson in life was how to recognise them.

I had read this book years before, but now that I had this new understanding of how my mind worked the book made sense. I had looked at property for years. As a child when my grandparents died and my parents moved house, through my own house purchases and near repossessions, watching my friends. I had been taking it all in and storing it for later, for when I was ready to process it consciously. And the time was now – I was ready.

The property journey begins

To step back a little, in 2004, after many years of disagreement about the actual investment strategy, my sister and I borrowed money from my parents and invested in a buy-to-let flat in London. We used the services of an experienced investor to buy the flat using a mortgage and then leased it to the council in return for rent. The rent was more than the cost of the mortgage and so we got to keep the profit. After a while, as house prices had risen, I remortgaged the flat and bought another and then repeated the process.

Then the world changed...

In 2007, I was aware that something was happening to the economy. I didn't understand what exactly, but knew I needed to pay attention. I started to listen to the news, watch current affairs programmes and have different types of conversations. I learnt that some people thought that the property market was going to crash, that prices would fall, in part because in economic terms they could not rise forever.

We all know that was just part of the story. Extraordinary banking practices called 'derivatives' meant that banks could sell 'bad debts' wrapped up in insurance policies to one another for profit. If you are interested in this extreme insanity, then read the three books by Dass, Morris and Rajan referenced in the Bibliography on page 103.

The world economy started to collapse as the weight of debt pressed. An easier read on a mind-blowing topic about the world of banking, finance and what you really need to know has been written by Simon Dixon called *Bank to the Future: Protect your future before the governments go bust*. The point is that if you lend to people who cannot repay you, then you don't have a business you have a liability, and that cannot go on for long.

I made the decision to remortgage the flats we had in London for one last time and pull out our equity (at effectively the height of the market). I didn't consider the impact of interest rate rises and I have to say we have been extremely lucky. These properties were such good investments that they managed to remain cashflowing even in the darkest days of the economy and at the height of the interest rates.

Property full time

In 2008, I decided to start investing in buy-to-let properties as a full-time career. The property prices were falling and I understood more about money than I ever had in my life. We even had a small London portfolio to whet our appetite.

As a family partnership, we all chipped £25,000 into a pot. We all got trained and then decided that I would do all the work as the others preferred the security of employment. In effect, my family became my first sourcing clients. Over the next year, I only managed to complete on the purchase of one property and I really struggled. The lessons taught by the property training companies had made it all seem so easy. The reality was much harder.

What none of my property training courses or books explained was how the changes in the economy would impact on anyone investing in property. This was my job, my business and it was under threat. No one predicted that banks would suffer so badly and that because of their past practices they would spiral into a period of lending shortages. The money traded on the markets between lenders (and then lent out to us at a profit) would virtually dry up, interest rates would first rise steeply as inter-lender confidence faltered. Interest rates would then fall to the lowest on record as the government had to intervene to control the risk of spiralling inflation.

Time to get serious

In November 2008, I made the decision that I was either going to be successful or go and work in the local supermarket stacking shelves at night. I set my goals and through my own determination set about buying one or two properties per month on average for myself or clients throughout 2009. By mid-2010, I had enough net rental income (profit) to cover my household expenses so that I would never have to have a 'normal' job again.

I published my first book and started the first of my two property businesses. I began to formally find (source) property deals for clients who had cash they wanted to invest in return for more money than they could get from the banks.

In the space between starting full-time property investment in late 2008 and the autumn of 2010, I had turned our family portfolio into a business worth over £2 million generating over £100,000 a year.

What does this have to do with the title of this book?

Watch what happened next?

Bob and my daughters have lived through my 'mind enhancing' last few years, like the saints they are. They listened and adapted as I spouted on about how we need to take responsibility for our own lives and not blame others. I will have shared a distilled version of that understanding with you as I explained the myths and the facts of life.

They also watched as I bought property after property. Bob visited properties with me and understood the concepts and the numbers involved. He started to become more involved in the business in 2009 – he had to as he was party to many of the mortgages we have. My younger daughter came along on the buying trips and saw the properties that we own. After all, in the end, the portfolios will all belong to her and her sister.

My elder daughter, Kimberley, was not interested. You cannot force your children to see how important this is – you have to be patient with them (this means start buying in your name and wait for them to ask what you are doing). Occasionally, we had conversations that hinted that she wanted me to buy her a house. I made it very clear that that was not how it worked. We invested our money to make a profit (a salary if you like). Houses in the south did not make sense from an investment point of view, especially when I could earn so much more by comparison by buying further north. From Case study 1 on page 78, you know what happened next...

The journey to help my child buy their own house

In 2010, Kimberley's questions started to change and became more about the concept of buying a house, what was needed and what was the process. I explained to her step by step the stages that she would need to go through. I shared this with you in an easy-to-understand way that is also easy to put into practice, if you so choose.

In early 2011, Kimberley started to actively look for a house. Again, I shared my knowledge and understanding of the market. I helped her to understand how to narrow and refine the searches. We started to view properties together and I explained what to look for and how to speak to vendors. What questions to ask and how to decide how much should be offered for each property.

Within months Kimberley had chosen the property she wanted and negotiated the purchase offer price. The next step was to fully embrace the mortgaging process. After a delay caused by the vendors, she moved into her first house in November 2011. By 2012, Kimberley was already discussing how she could buy a second property for investment purposes – and so increase her monthly income.

Please let this be the start of us helping to create financial security by understanding the part that *Property for the Next Generation* can play for all our families.

Bibliography

Publications

Canfield, J. (et al) (2009) *Chicken Soup for the Entrepreneur's Soul: Advice and Inspiration on Fulfilling Dreams*, Health Communications.

Dass, S. (2010) *Traders, Guns and Money: Knowns and Unknowns in the Dazzling World of Derivatives*, FT/Prentice Hall.

Dixon, S. (2012) *Bank to the Future: Protect Your Future Before Governments Go Bust*, Searching Finance Ltd.

Evans, T. (2010) *Flavours of Thoughts: recipes for fresh thinking*, Tom Evans, UK.

Evans, T. (2011) *The Art and Science of Light Bulb Moments*, O Books, UK.

Hill, N. (1960) *Think and Grow Rich*, Highroads.

Howard, C. (2005) *Turning Passions Into Profits: Three Steps to Wealth and Power*, John Wiley & Sons.

Howard, C. (2009) *Instant Wealth Wake up Rich!: Discover The Secret of The New Entrepreneurial Mind*, John Wiley & Sons.

Kiyosaki, R. (2002) *Rich Dad Poor Dad: What the Rich Teach Their Kids About Money That the Poor and Middle Class Do Not!* Time Warner.

Kiyosaki, R. (2009) *Rich Dad's Conspiracy of The Rich: The 8 New Rules of Money*, Hachette.

Kiyosaki, R. (2011) *Unfair Advantage: The Power of Financial Education*, Plata Publishing.

Maslow, Abraham H. (Kindle version 2011) *Hierarchy of Needs: A Theory of Human Motivation.*

Massey, M. (1979) *The People Puzzle*, Reston Publishing (A Prentice Hall Co).

Maxwell, J. C. (2007) *The 21 Irrefutable Laws of Leadership: Follow Them and People Will Follow You*, Thomas Nelson.

Metcalf, F. (2003) *Buddha in your Backpack*, Ulysses Press, USA.

Morris, C. R. (2009) *Two Trillion Dollar Meltdown: Easy Money, High Rollers, and the Great Credit Crash*, PublicAffairs.

Olson, J. (2005) *The Slight Edge: Turning Simple Disciplines into Massive Success*, Momentum Media.

Power, P. (2009) *Know Me, Like Me, Follow Me: What Online Social Networking Means for You and Your Business*, Headline Business Plus.

Priestley, D. (2010) *Become a Key Person of Influence*, Ecademy Press.

Rajan, R. G. (2011) *Fault Lines: How Hidden Fractures Still Threaten the World Economy*, Princeton University Press.

Redfield, J. (1994) *The Celestine Prophecy*, Bantam.

Rohn, J. (1993) *The Art of Exceptional Living* [Audiobook], Nightingale Conant.

Singer, B. (2008) *Little Voice Mastery: How to Win the War Between Your Ears in 30 Seconds or Less and Have an Extraordinary Life*, Xcel Holdings.

Trump, D. and Kiyosaki, R. (2006) *Why We Want You to Be Rich: Two Men – One Message*, Rich Press.

Upton, D. (2009) *Create Your Desires and Fulfill Your Dreams*, UKUnpublished.

Weerasinghe, R. Dr (2011) *Turning Point: A 6 Step Process for Transforming Your Life*, Ecademy Press.

Wusche, V. (2012) *Using Other People's Money: How to invest in property*, SRA Books.

Wusche, V. (2012) *Make More Money from Property: From investor thinking to a business mindset*, SRA Books

Weblinks

www.TheSourcersApprentice.com

www.ThePropertySourcers.com

e-book

Wusche, V. (2012) *Managing Your Credit Cards, Scores and Reports.*

Moving forward...

Programmes, products and services

I believe it is my purpose in life to share knowledge and, in doing so, inspire and educate people so that they can identify and leverage their previously untapped personal resources. Together, we will create generations of financially secure business owners and property investors and turn our economy back from recession.

I have the writing bug and I will continue to create a variety of books, blogs, products, services and events.

You will find many free resources on my websites, including a free newsletter focused on financial news, property investment and wealth creation.

Visit: www.ThePropertyMermaid.com and www.TheSourcersApprentice.com.

Vicki Wusche

Since 1994, Vicki has shared her knowledge and understanding of all things entrepreneurial, wealth and personal development. She has trained or spoken in front of thousands of people across the UK.

During her time working at a high level to influence education policy and teaching, Vicki worked with inspirational entrepreneurs at the cutting edge of

a new media revolution, while at the same time supporting some of the most deprived people in London through her work as director for two charitable organisations focused on regeneration, housing, refugees, employment and re-inspiring young people.

Throughout her time working in education, and more recently in property investment and wealth creation, Vicki has constantly studied both formally and informally the great minds, concepts and strategies vital to business success. This has led to a Master's degree, a Diploma in Higher Education and a Master NLP qualification to mention but a few.

In September 2010, Vicki published her first book *Using Other People's Money: How to Invest in Property*. By March 2012, she was celebrating the launch of *Make More Money from Property: From Investor Thinking to a Business Mindset*, her eagerly awaited second book. In September 2012, her first book was re-published in a new edition– a complete rewrite with new case studies and strategies. Finally, *Property for the Next Generation*, her third book, has been written for the general public rather than those already in property circles.

Throughout her employment or entrepreneurial endeavours, the driving forces behind Vicki are her family and her desire to help others maximise the resources they have, be they mental, emotional, financial or physical.

Combining all her skills and experience, with an ability to translate complex concepts with passion into everyday practicalities, Vicki is focused on building property portfolios for clients who have access to financial resources. Vicki's clients recognise that this is a once-in-a-generation opportunity to build long-lasting financial security for their families and to secure and leverage their hard-earned wages before inflation erodes them. The clients, however, simply lack the time to take advantage – that's where Vicki's experience and service comes into play.

Together with her business partners, Vicki offers a range of support for those looking to build their own business in property or expand their commercial businesses.

Property for the Next Generation is Vicki Wusche's third book.

Her first, *Using Other People's Money: How to invest in property*, was published in 2010 and explains the principals of using other people's money to buy property. The book takes the reader through a series of provoking chapters, which demonstrate the concept of exploring alternative funding avenues and, by revisiting the use of credit and assessing existing assets, could lead to an exciting property portfolio and a regular income. The book was so successful that it sold out within the first year and was republished as a fully updated and revised edition in autumn 2012.

Vicki's second book, *Make More Money from Property: From investor thinking to a business mindset* had outstanding reviews when launched in London in March 2012. Vicki explores the property market and challenges the reader to change from investor thinking to a business mindset. The reader is encouraged to take further steps towards a future that is financially free by re-examining current investment opportunities, and understanding the way money can be used to make more money. Why are the rich getting richer, and how can you apply that thinking to your own life?

An excellent and absorbing trilogy of literature, written in a style that is easy to break down, analyse and absorb, and which fundamentally makes good investment and business sense – the books are available as a bundle at: http://bit.ly/MMMFPL and in Kindle version on Amazon.

'I finished *Using Other People's Money: How to invest in property* this morning [after reading *Make More Money from Property: From investor thinking to a business mindset*]. I really found both of your books a fantastic read with plenty of gold nuggets to take away. So thank you for the great value you've added to my life, looking forward to reading your next book!'

Luke S

'Unlike many property books, Vicki doesn't just talk about strategies. She talks more about realising what I want from my life and how property can get me there. I like Vicki's philosophy. When I was stuck in my business I turned to Vicki for some coaching. Before I met her, I had not properly "joined the dots". I would spend hours, if not days, being in my head and not getting anywhere.

After a Personal Investment Planning session, Vicki clearly showed me the way forward, reinforcing my beliefs and setting out a course of action. I am now clear on my path, my business model and my actions to get me there. I have so much to do now and lots of actions I know will get me where I want to be. I also learnt some mindset strategies along the way. Thank you, Vicki, for unblocking me.'

Nick B

'Read your book three times and got more out of it each time. I realise now that I was blinkered. I thought I had to save for three years and buy a place in Clapham for a capital return – thank you – can I work with you?'

James K

The Property Sourcers

- Your home is not an asset!
- Your pension is not enough!

For those of you who are asset or equity rich but time poor, this is your opportunity to build wealth! After experiencing a personalised strategy session, your financial and investment plan will be clearly defined. Depending on your circumstances, personal choice and financial situation, we can take the hard work out of investing for you. We will produce and fully micro-manage an investment portfolio strategy on your behalf, which will allow you to reap the benefits and financial rewards without the effort!

creating your property nest egg

Since 2009, Vicki has been using her experience and knowledge of the property market to build cashflowing property portfolios for bespoke clients. Offering ROI of over 10%,[35] the properties that Vicki sources are identified to generate cashflow and create financial security for clients, leaving them to focus on their lives.

The process will start with us working together to develop your personal investment plan in a one-to-one strategy session. During two and a half hours, Vicki works with you to help you recognise the pros and cons of property investment, your personal investment goals and identify a clear investment strategy. While the majority of clients (over 80%) go on to invest

---

35 ROI depends on your personal financial circumstances and the mortgages available at the time.

with Vicki and her team, this is not a sales pitch. You will leave with a clear investment strategy that enables you to make the right investment choices, at the right time, for you.

With the development of The Property Sourcers, Vicki and her partners can now work with a discrete group of cash-rich investors offering a hands-free process designed to balance the investor's needs for security and flexibility with a busy life.

This service is not for everyone: clients will need to pass credit checks, have a provable income and have access to financial resources. Professional advice will be provided throughout the process through a team of experts in the property, tax and financial world.

With lending criteria becoming increasingly challenging, please contact Vicki and her team to arrange a free, no-obligation call to assess whether this programme suits your needs and circumstances and takes away your worries and concerns. Then book your strategy session to determine your Readiness to Invest.

For further information on this service, visit www.ThePropertySourcers.com or email me at ask@ThePropertySourcers.com to arrange your personalised 'Ready to Invest' strategy session.

The Sourcer's Apprentice

The Sourcers Apprentice programmes consist of audio, video and workbook solutions to help you rapidly build a successful property investment business. Join us with this informative, in-depth and incredibly valuable multi-learning tool, which takes you from the fundamental inspiration stage right through on a step-by-step learning process to the successful creation of your own personalised business model.

Providing you and your children with all the documents, research tools, dos and don'ts, plus hand-holding instructional information to enable you to become a highly effective, cashflowing and profitable property sourcer.

Vicki and Loran are both qualified teachers and want to develop their materials in a way in which young people can understand. Their first 'product' is a series of events that combine experiential learning with traditional teaching called 'The Next Generation Adventures'. Please contact us if you would like more information.

The books, videos and audios enable people to use the learning outlined in this book and in *Make More Money from Property: From Investor Thinking to a Business Mindset* and take it to another level.

For more information contact ask@TheSourcersApprentice.com.

We have created a website to support you and your family as you work through this book and the ideas contained in it.

Property for the Next Generation

Please find new resources freely available to support you as well as information about events I recommend and attend.

Our aim is to continue to create online resources to support you in taking personal responsibility for your own financial future, and give you access to new information as it becomes available.

If you have any questions or ideas please email us at ask@PropertyForTheNextGeneration.com